Igniting the Spark

spark /spärk/ *noun* A small fleck of gold

IGNITING THE SPARK

THE PURSUIT of GOLD IN CALIFORNIA

Ort J. Lofthus

with L. Gianforte

BLUEFIG
PUBLISHING

Cover and book design by Kevin Yee, kevinyeedesign.com

Photos courtesy of Bank of Stockton
Historical Photograph Collection

ISBN: 978-0-578-57047-1

Library of Congress Control Number: 2019914860

DEDICATION

*For my wife, Sylvia, who was always by my side
and will forever be in my heart*

ACKNOWLEDGMENTS

I am grateful to my dear friends, Maury and Hope Kane, who went gleefully into the foothills of California's Gold Country to research and write more than 200 stories at my request. These stories, each of them one minute long, were prepared for broadcasting for radio stations KJOY and KJAX in Stockton. They were creative, ingenious, and exciting. These tales truly came to life thanks to the resonant voice of narrator Franklin Wilbur, who served as director of the theater department at San Joaquin Delta College for seventeen years.

I extend special thanks to the Bank of Stockton. At the inception of this project three decades ago, the Bank of Stockton underwrote the broadcasting of the stories. When I approached the current president, Douglass M. Eberhardt II, with the idea for this book, the bank's generosity once again shone brightly. I appreciate the steady hand of Angela Brusa, vice president of marketing for the Bank of Stockton. Her contributions and suggestions have proved invaluable in every phase of producing this book. In particular, her introduction to me of our editor and publisher, Elle Gianforte, of Blue Fig Creative/Publishing, turned out to be another nugget of gold. Elle has been our beacon in guiding us to this final product. I consider her a lifelong friend.

My deepest appreciation to Kevin Yee for his flawless talent in designing this book, and to William Maxwell, archivist for the Bank of Stockton, who selected all the photos to beautifully illustrate the stories.

I am especially grateful to my family, who encouraged me to bring this book to life despite the personal tragedy of losing my wife, Sylvia, the love of my life for seventy-two years.

CONTENTS

FOREWORD

This book is a true collaboration. With roots dating back nearly forty years, its origins lie in the vision of two Stockton businessmen who wished to share the tales of California's Gold Rush with their community.

In 1980, my uncle, Bob Eberhardt, who was then the 7th president of the Bank of Stockton, joined forces with his friend, Ort Lofthus, co-owner and general manager of KJOY-KJAX radio, to bring California's rich history to life. The bank was among the station's underwriters, and the two men enjoyed a successful working relationship.

Committed to both entertaining and informing listeners, they conceived the idea of enhancing the station's format by including stories of the Mother Lode. They partnered with Ken Fong Advertising, the bank's ad agency, to create the California Heritage Series—a collection of 60-second radio spots depicting the early days of California, which delighted local audiences. Each story opened with an introduction by narrator Franklin Wilbur: "The Bank of Stockton, withstanding the test of time since 1867, presents another colorful tale from the early days of California."

At that time, the Bank of Stockton—the area's largest and oldest community bank—had eight branches and $300 million dollars in assets. KJOY-KJAX was the local radio station that covered the bank's main market areas in San Joaquin County. For more than a decade, the partnership proved beneficial to both organizations. Given the bank's history as the oldest financial institution in the state of California still operating under its original charter, the project turned out to be a natural fit for us.

In early 2019, when Ort reached out to me to see if I had any interest in helping him produce this book, I was more than happy to help. The idea of being able to reintroduce the stories and preserve them for perpetuity seemed like a very worthwhile project.

Uncle Bob passed away in 1994, but he would be so pleased to see that Ort had brought these stories back to life in the pages of this book. He would also be thrilled to know that our Bank of Stockton Archives, established under his leadership in 1990, served as a photo resource to illustrate the book. Bob, like Ort, would have wanted people to remember the fascinating history that created the community we call home.

Today, the Bank of Stockton has twenty branches in sixteen cities spanning nine counties, with assets standing strong at $3.3 billion dollars. Our archives house more than 40,000 historical photos from the Central Valley, the Mother Lode, and surrounding communities, and continues to be a valuable resource for the region.

The original collaboration between the Bank of Stockton and KJOY-KJAX in presenting these stories to the public many years ago is a testament to both entities' commitment to preserving the past for generations to come. We thank Ort for giving us the opportunity to participate in this special project.

We hope you enjoy this culmination of friendship, business, and a love of history that inspired the creation of *Igniting the Spark*.

Douglass M. Eberhardt II
9th President, CEO, and Chairman of the Board
Bank of Stockton

PREFACE
THE ORIGINS OF THIS BOOK

From the late 1960s through the mid 1980s, I commissioned journalist Maury Kane to write a series of stories about California's Gold Rush. His wife, Hope Kane, conducted the research, and together they created a rich and colorful picture of life in the Mother Lode in the mid-1800s. Their stories were produced by my radio station, KJOY-KJAX in Stockton, and originally aired as approximately sixty-second vignettes underwritten by the Bank of Stockton.

Since then, I have entertained the vision of consolidating and editing some of these tales—plus a few new ones for good measure—into a single manuscript. My wish was to give readers a glimpse into the past, bringing the landscape of the era and the lives of the Forty-Niners into vivid perspective. This book was born from that dream.

INTRODUCTION
A Brief Overview of the California Gold Rush

It began as an ordinary winter morning on January 24, 1848 in Coloma, California. By day's end, it would prove to mark the start of one of the most pivotal eras in the history of the United States. On that date, James W. Marshall discovered gold at Sutter's Mill—an event that launched an explosion of population and wealth in California.

The Gold Rush attracted more than 300,000 prospectors to the region, drawing them from throughout the world in their quest for fortune. Miners from Oregon, Hawaii, Mexico, South America, Europe, Great Britain, Australia, and China poured into the state—all focused on instant wealth. Between 1848 and 1859, they collectively unearthed more than 750,000 pounds of gold—valued at tens of billions in today's dollars.

The gold was found in the ground and panned from streams. Dug out of riverbeds and blasted from hillsides. Extracted from quartz and other rocks. Its high concentration in California is believed to have been the result of geologic actions that took place over the course of hundreds of millions of years.

FINDING WEALTH
In spite of the seemingly endless presence of gold, only a small number of fortune-seekers actually realized their dreams in the mines. While a few men struck it rich—changing their lives forever—others returned home with little more than what they had at the outset.

Fortunately for many, gold wasn't the only source of profit in the Mother Lode. Individuals with a true entrepreneurial spirit succeeded by providing services to the prospectors, such as food, whiskey, supplies, accommodations, and entertainment.

TRANSFORMING THE NATION
The discovery of gold in California had far-reaching effects. It opened the West to unparalleled development, facilitating California's rise to statehood. It also shored up the nation's economy, and many historians believe that the United States could not have survived the financial shock of the Civil War had it not been for the gold from the Mother Lode.

HISTORY MAKERS:
Men of the Gold Country

≈>●<≈

James W. Marshall

Born in New Jersey in 1810, James Wilson Marshall followed in his father's footsteps and pursued his trade as a carpenter. When he was in his late teens he headed west, eventually settling as a farmer in Kansas. In 1844, a bout of malaria led him to join a wagon train bound for Oregon, where he hoped to improve his health.

A year later, Marshall made his way to California and returned to his carpentry roots. He entered into a partnership with John Sutter to build a water-powered sawmill on the banks of the American River in Coloma, California, where he is credited with being the first to discover gold.

This quote, attributed to Marshall, appears in The California Gold Country: Highway 49 Revisited by Elliot H. Koeppel:

"One morning in January —it was a clear, cold morning; I shall never forget that morning—as I was taking my usual walk along the race after shutting off the water, my eye was caught with the glimpse of something shining in the bottom of the ditch. There was about a foot of water running then. I reached my hand down and picked it up; it made my heart thump, for I was certain it was gold."

In spite of his momentous discovery, Marshall did not fare well. He was unable to obtain any legal credit for his claims in the goldfields, and the sawmill failed when most of the workers focused their energies on the pursuit of gold. He left the area and drifted throughout California, eventually living out the rest of his life in a sparse cabin.

John Augustus Sutter

John Sutter

In 1839, thirty-six-year-old John Augustus Sutter arrived in California to seek his fortune. He obtained three ships in San Francisco—then called Yerba Buena—and loaded them with supplies, then sailed to the settlement now known as Sacramento. There he and the Native Americans he used for labor built an adobe-walled fortress, Sutter's Fort, which became a busy trading post.

When his business partner, James Marshall, found gold near their sawmill in Coloma in 1848, the discovery brought Sutter nothing but trouble. Although space was rented at his fort for stores, boarding houses, and saloons, many men borrowed from the generous Sutter and never repaid him.

Plagued by squatters and burdened with the heavy costs of defending his land titles, Sutter gave up his fort. It deteriorated rapidly, and was purchased by public subscription and given to the state of California in 1890. Today, restored as a state historical monument, Sutter's Fort provides a link to the lively history of early California—and serves as a shrine to a man and his shattered dreams.

I feel it is important to note here that the statue of John Sutter at 28th and L streets in Sacramento was recently removed by Sutter Health, which operates a medical campus near that location, due to historical accounts of Sutter's abuse of Native Americans.

John Bidwell

The party of pioneers that crossed the Sierra into California in 1841 included twenty-two-year-old John Bidwell, a quiet young man who was destined to leave his mark on the future of the Golden State.

A few years before arriving in California, Bidwell had decided to settle down on 160 acres of farmland in Missouri. When a claim jumper moved in, however, Bidwell opted to move on. He was driven not by lack of courage to confront the man, but by the fact that he was underage and in no position to contest the action in court. Little did he realize at the time that his true destiny lay nearly 2,000 miles to the west.

Soon after his arrival in New Helvetia, now Sacramento, Bidwell went to work as the business manager for John Sutter and eventually became overseer of Sutter's extensive property holdings. In time, he bought the 22,000-acre Rancho Arroyo Chico, where his progressive farming and cattle-raising methods brought him a fortune.

Bidwell was a delegate to the national convention of the Democratic Party in 1860. He switched parties four years later and served as a delegate to the national convention of the Republican Party in 1864. That same year, he was elected to Congress.

Bidwell ran for governor of California in 1875 on the Anti-Monopoly Party ticket and again in 1880 on the Prohibition ticket. Given his popularity, he could well have been elected, but his high principles prevented him from making any political deals. As one newspaper correspondent wrote, "He is too good a man to be governor."

After Bidwell's death in 1899 at the age of eighty, it was said of him, "He would have made Diogenes' quest for any honest man easy."

John McMillin

A quiet country lane bearing his name and an unassuming grave in Stockton Rural Cemetery are the only visible vestiges of one of San Joaquin County's most courageous and philanthropic pioneers, Captain John McMillin.

His spirit of adventure took root in 1839 at the early age of fifteen, when he ran away from his home in Tallahassee, Florida, to join the Texas Rangers. His bravery in battle soon earned him the rank of captain, but his glory days were clouded when he and his 180-man unit were captured during the war between Texas and Mexico.

After an unsuccessful escape attempt from their prison in Mexico City, they tried again and ultimately managed to flee on horseback. Unbeknownst to the intrepid group, however, Mexican guards had learned of their plan and ambushed them as they rode through a narrow pass. When gunfire struck one of the Rangers and killed his horse, McMillin turned his steed around to save the injured man, throwing him over his saddle. This bold act of bravery so impressed the guards that they stopped shooting and applauded, allowing the Americans to escape. McMillin later received a silver belt from the Mexican general, Santa Ana, in recognition of his valor.

In time, the pull of the Gold Rush lured McMillin to California, but it was his success as a cattle rancher in southern San Joaquin County that defined his fortune. As legend goes, he once advanced a young butcher's apprentice 900 head of cattle to help him get started in the ranching industry. The boy, Henry Miller, grew to become a partner in the Miller-Lux Ranch, boasting more than one million head of cattle on the county's west side. McMillin was amply repaid for his generosity.

Stories abound about McMillin's laissez-faire nature—a trait that served him well. He once came upon several men who were camping illegally on a remote section of his 30,000-acre ranch. He recognized the leader as the famous bandit Joaquin Murrieta, known as the Robin Hood of the West. Concerned for his family's safety, he did nothing to disturb the outlaw and his band. Afterward, Murrieta showed up at McMillin's

11

home and paid in gold for the cattle that he and his men had eaten. This soon became a pattern, with the group often camping on the ranch and dutifully paying for the livestock they consumed.

Over time, McMillin went on to organize the first San Joaquin County Fair Association and build Stockton's first theater. True to his entrepreneurial spirit, he also started several businesses. He was only forty-four when he died of typhoid fever, which he contracted by drinking water from the San Joaquin River.

Reuel Colt Gridley monument in Stockton Rural Cemetery

Reuel Colt Gridley

In 1864, Reuel Colt Gridley was a shopkeeper in the small town of Austin, Nevada. During that year's mayoral campaign, he and a friend agreed that if their candidate lost, the loser would carry a fifty-pound sack of flour through the town. Gridley's candidate did not prevail, so he honored the bet.

When he finished his trek, an enterprising observer suggested that the flour be auctioned off to raise money for the Civil War's wounded soldiers. The winner declined to take the bag, and instead returned it to Gridley so it could be auctioned off again. And again. And again.

Gridley and his flour sack traveled to the cities and mining camps of Nevada and California, then headed east for additional auctions in major cities. By the time the bidding finally ended, Gridley had raised $275,000 by selling and reselling a single sack of flour. He became known as The Soldier's Friend, and he moved to Stockton, California two years later.

Gridley died in November of 1870 and was buried in a common grave under a simple cross in the community he grew to love. Seventeen years after his death, a monument was dedicated in his honor in Stockton Rural Cemetery. Gridley is depicted with his hand resting on the notorious fifty-pound sack of flour. Today, that monument is a state landmark that stands as a tribute to the greatness of a humble humanitarian.

John Marsh residence near Brentwood

John Marsh

The specter of John Marsh still haunts the isolated mountain known as Diablo in California's Contra Costa County. It was along its eastern slopes that this complex man built an empire.

Marsh arrived in California in 1836 and promptly began practicing medicine, passing off his Harvard University bachelor's degree as a medical degree. The fact that he had previously trained as an assistant to two physicians helped him accomplish the ruse.

Despite his lack of formal credentials, Marsh apparently practiced good medicine. His fees, on the other hand, were atrociously high. He often demanded payment of twenty-five cows for a professional visit—fifty cows if he had to remain overnight.

In time, Marsh accumulated enough wealth to buy a 50,000-acre cattle ranch in the Mount Diablo foothills. Among his guests were members of the Bartleson-Bidwell Party, the first American emigrants to attempt a wagon crossing from Missouri to California.

Although Marsh was not known for his generosity, he opened his purse strings for Abigail Tuck, a Massachusetts schoolteacher who won his heart. After only a two-week courtship, the two were married in 1851.

Shortly afterward, Marsh started construction on his ultimate gift to her: the largest and most expensive stone mansion in all of California. While this might seem to be the perfect fairy-tale ending to their story, it was not to be. Abigail died of tuberculosis in 1855, before the house was completed. Marsh eventually moved into the house on his own. Three weeks later, he was stabbed to death by three of his vaqueros in an argument over their pay.

Ben Buster

A formerly enslaved man, Ben Buster headed to the Mother Lode town of Mokelumne Hill, California, when he managed to escape. It was there that he discovered gold, changing the direction of his life forever.

When his successful claim began to fade, Buster moved on to San Antone Camp in Calaveras County. A storekeeper in town weighed his gold, estimating its value at $40,000.

Buster used his newfound wealth to buy his freedom, and twice he bought the freedom of his parents. The first time, the slaveholder pocketed the money. The second time, Buster hired an attorney who made certain the two were released. Sadly, their freedom came too late. Both of Buster's parents died on their way to California.

The extent of Buster's wealth was widely known, and it was believed that his treasure was buried near his cabin in Red Gulch. Twice, the same two men tortured him in an attempt to get him to reveal where his gold was hidden. In both instances the men were captured—first given fifty lashes and then hanged.

Buster often warned that if anyone found his gold after he died, his spirit would haunt them for the rest of their lives. This admonition fell on deaf ears, because after his death, treasure hunters tore his cabin apart in search of his gold. Mediums tried to communicate with Buster's spirit to determine his secret hiding place, but Buster wasn't talking.

His spirit remains untroubled today on the hill above the cabin site where his mortal remains are buried. As far as anyone knows, Buster's gold is still where he hid it.

George C. Vail

One of the most remarkable judges during California's Gold Rush era was George C. Vail, who hailed from the town of Yreka. His judicial decisions were totally unencumbered by legal training, but what he lacked in law he made up for in common sense.

One day, a young miner entered Judge Vail's courtroom and charged that his employer had just left town without paying his wages for an entire winter's work. Taking two constables with him, the judge personally took off after the fleeing boss. The man was apprehended and returned to the courtroom, where he acknowledged the debt but claimed he had no money to repay it.

"Constable," ordered Vail, "take this man and stand him on his head, then shake him up and listen if you can hear anything drop."

Out of the allegedly impoverished employer's pockets fell a bag of gold dust that was deemed to be worth $2,000.

Vail promptly decreed that the chagrined defendant pay his former employee his back wages—plus give the two constables and the judge himself an ounce of gold dust each for their time and trouble in bringing him to justice. The judge then ordered that the man be placed right-side up—and released.

Charles E. Boles, aka Black Bart

Charles Earl Boles

Stories about the highwaymen of the Gold Rush would not be complete without mentioning the English-born Charles Earl Boles, more commonly known as Black Bart. Dubbed the Gentleman Bandit, he robbed more than two dozen Wells Fargo stagecoaches in Northern California without ever firing a shot.

Black Bart always worked solo, carried an unloaded gun, and traveled on foot. He was renowned for his style, sophistication, and courteous manner, refusing to steal women's jewelry and focusing only on money. His signature became his habit of placing an original poem in the strong-boxes he emptied, one of which went like this:

"So blame me not for what I've done,
I don't deserve your curses,
And if for any cause I'm hung,
Let it be for my verses."

Boles was shot in the hand during his last robbery attempt at Funk Hill in Calaveras County. Although he fled the scene, he left behind a bloody handkerchief whose laundry mark was eventually traced to an establishment in San Francisco. He was convicted of the final robbery, sentenced to six years in San Quentin, and released after four years for good behavior.

When reporters asked him if he planned to return to robbing stages, Boles replied, "No, gentlemen. I'm through with crime."

William Wingfield

A self-professed inventor, William Wingfield caused a considerable stir when he arrived in a little Mother Lode mining town near Auburn, California. He claimed to have created a divining rod that could unerringly pinpoint the precise location of gold far beneath the earth's surface.

Eager to tap into the power of this amazing invention, nine prospectors paid Wingfield $100 each to show them where they could strike gold in Little Annie Ledge, a granite outcropping that had, to date, produced little more than black sand. Near a clump of Manzanita, Wingfield's divining rod dipped wildly downward. The men began digging frantically, and on the second day, Little Annie's investors struck a pocket that yielded $2,400 in gold.

Wingfield was well out of town when a delegation of miners overtook him and persuaded him, at gunpoint, to return and repeat his feat.

This time, Wingfield demanded $500 from each miner for his detecting services, and they willingly obliged. A few days later, the divining rod dipped again at a new location, causing mass excitement among the prospectors. When their digging produced nothing but granite, the angry investors marched Wingfield off to jail.

He was given a thirty-day sentence to await the outcome of exploration on the mine that the prospectors had prophetically named the Last Chance. When it proved a failure, the hapless Wingfield was tried by a jury, speedily convicted, and hanged. His divining rod was awarded to the jury foreman, one of six jurors from whom Wingfield had collected $500.

Ah Lin

The history of the Calaveras County mining town of Jenny Lind is inextricably linked to Ah Lin. One of approximately 500 Chinese miners who painstakingly sifted the sands along the Calaveras River for gold, he spent sixty years in the town and was a friend to everyone.

According to tradition, when a person from China died in the Mother Lode, his remains were to be shipped to his homeland for burial. Ah Lin, however, made it clear that he wished to be buried among his American friends, whom he had grown to cherish as family.

Ah Lin's close friend, Abraham Rosenberg—a wealthy San Francisco fruit shipper who was born and raised in Jenny Lind—preceded him in death. In his will, he left provisions for Ah Lin's last days and for a tombstone on his grave. When Ah Lin died at the age of 100, he was laid to rest with all the dignity and reverence due such a grand man.

Charles M. Weber, founder of Stockton

Charles M. Weber

Stockton's founder, Captain Charles M. Weber, was impressed that March day in 1848 when he examined specimens of gold brought to him by a prospector in Tuleburg, as the town of Stockton was then called. The samples were from the American River near Sutter's Mill, where James W. Marshall had discovered gold just two months earlier. There was considerable skepticism throughout the state about the value of Marshall's find, but Weber was encouraged by what he saw.

So confident was he that he staked his last dollar on organizing an expedition that went on to find gold in every stream from the Mokelumne River to the American River. What's more, the samples he found were richer than anything Marshall had unearthed.

Weber subsequently arranged for another expedition that was equally successful. Its gold discoveries resulted in the establishment of many important Mother Lode camps south of the Mokelumne River. The explorations of Stockton's founding father likely did more to hasten California's Gold Rush than Marshall's discovery or any subsequent excursions.

Charles Weber knew it was critical for him to negotiate a treaty with the chief of the much-feared Siyakumna Indians. Without it, he had little chance of colonizing his Spanish land grant that stretched from Stockton to French Camp, about six miles to the south.

The year was 1843. Weber had arranged a meeting at Sutter's Fort with Chief José Jesús, whose tribe claimed the territory in the Weber grant. The negotiations were successful, and the chief agreed to defend Weber's new settlers against the Mexicans, whom he despised, and against other Indians.

As a result of this peaceful settlement, a lasting friendship developed between Weber and Jesús. When Jesús was seriously hurt in a fight with a man in Stockton six years later, Weber sent his own physician to save the chief's life. In honor of their bond, Weber had a Stockton street named after his friend. Several years later, however, the name of the street was changed to honor a hero of the day, General Ulysses S. Grant.

The life of Charles Weber and the future of Stockton hung in doubt during an exceedingly grim period in 1846. The war with Mexico had broken out, and Weber was taken prisoner by Mexican authorities. His dream of colonizing his Spanish land grant seemed remote.

Twice he was taken from his cell to be shot; twice his life was spared at the last minute.

Just as unexpectedly, Weber was released by the Mexican forces as they neared the Colorado River in their journey from California to Mexico. He made his way to Los Angeles, where he formed a friendship with Robert Field Stockton, the United States military commander. In time, his name would be given to Weber's new city.

Downtown Stockton's business district might have developed in a much different fashion had it not been for a waterfront accident and a directional glitch.

As the founder of Stockton, Charles Weber had always planned that the center of the young city's commerce would be the north side of Miner Channel. There, with a peninsula extending into the harbor, ships could

Weber residence on McLeod Lake and Stockton Channel, circa 1850

sail up the channel and unload their goods virtually at the back doors of the shops that Weber was certain would be built there. Alas, his strategic plan was not to be.

While executing plans for his general store, Weber directed the captain of a sailing ship to unload the lumber for the building on the north side of the channel. For reasons unknown to this day, the captain delivered the lumber to the channel's south side.

Some pioneers claimed that the captain ran his ship aground on the south bank, and was therefore forced to unload. Others claim that he merely misunderstood Weber's instructions. Whatever the cause, the damage was done, because there was no immediate means of moving the lumber to the opposite side of the waterway.

Weber's general store was ultimately erected on the south bank, setting the pattern and direction for downtown Stockton's future growth.

———————

The year was 1850, and Charles Weber was fighting mad.

Too many of the Stockton's new oak trees were being needlessly cut down, and he was up in arms. In a newspaper announcement, he warned the public that anyone found felling trees on land other than their own would be prosecuted.

As time passed, Weber's stewardship of the trees was further demonstrated by his gift to the city of ten blocks of land to be used as public parks. Today, they serve as verdant monuments to Weber's foresight.

George Madeira

A state historical monument on a hill overlooking the Mother Lode mining town of Volcano honors the memory of one of its most illustrious sons. He was George Madeira, who arrived in Volcano in 1852 at the age of fifteen. In the quest for a better life, he and his family left Hagerstown, Maryland, but his mother fell victim to the tortuous trip and died on the prairie.

A budding astronomer, young George brought with him a box containing books, sky charts, and maps. Several times during the trip, his father threw the box out of the wagon to lighten the load on the oxen, but George always managed to retrieve it. In fact, he traveled most of the way on foot so his precious box could ride.

Upon arrival in Volcano, George came across a hill just outside of town that proved to be an ideal place to set up an observatory—the first amateur astronomical observatory in the state. It was from this vantage point that he used a three-inch refractor telescope to discover the Great Comet of 1861. (At the time, he wasn't aware that Australian John Tebbutt had discovered the comet more than a month earlier.)

Madeira went on to become a famous mining engineer, geologist, historian, and philosopher, but he never lost his interest in astronomy. In fact, it was he who encouraged multimillionaire James Lick to contribute $700,000 for the establishment of an observatory on Mount Hamilton, just east of San Jose. Today, the Lick Observatory is owned and operated by the University of California—and Volcano's Observatory Hill still attracts and inspires amateur astronomers.

Joaquin Murrieta

Joaquin Murrieta

The town of Murphys was said to be one of the favorite haunts of the Mother Lode bandit, Joaquin Murrieta. It was also one of the few places where he could find a barber with nerve enough to shave him.

As legend goes, Murrieta would walk into a barbershop and calmly say, "I want a shave. I will pay you a dollar for the shave, but if you cut me, I will kill you."

Apparently, the Murphys barber willing to accept these outrageous terms was as tough as Murrieta. When asked by a friend why he would dare to take such chances, he picked up his razor, ran his thumb along the sharp blade, and grinned.

"I do not take chances," he replied. "If I ever cut Joaquin, he will never get up out of the chair. I will give him one more cut—and he will be a very dead Joaquin."

Knight's Ferry, circa 1925, visited by Ulysses S. Grant in 1854

Ulysses S. Grant

Ulysses S. Grant visited California for the first time in 1852, seventeen years before being elected president. At the time, he was a young Army lieutenant commanding a regiment of soldiers bound for San Francisco by way of the Isthmus of Panama.

When Grant and his unit boarded the steamer Golden Gate in Panama City, a cholera epidemic was sweeping the region. Many of his men and several civilian passengers were already stricken. The first night, thirty-two soldiers died. The ship's captain was afraid to put out to sea, and there was no relief to be found on shore. As a result, the vessel was converted into a hospital ship until the epidemic subsided.

Grant personally nursed many of the sick. One soldier recalled that Grant was "a ministering angel to all of us."

Caring for the afflicted was not the only task Grant took on. When some of the enlisted men tried to desert, he stood guard at the gangway to prevent them from leaving. By the time the ship weighed anchor for San Francisco, eighty-four soldiers and civilians had died.

Grant went on to become commander of the Union forces in the Civil War and president of the United States, but his life was marked dramatically by the ordeal he experienced in the harbor of Panama City.

Levi Strauss

Levi Strauss is a classic example of a Gold Rush success story that did not originate in the mines.

Born in Bavaria, Strauss immigrated to New York in 1848 and joined his two brothers in their wholesale dry-goods company. When he heard about the discovery of gold in California, he headed to San Francisco and started his own branch of the family business. Initially, he sold textiles and other items to small stores.

Several years later, he was contacted by one of his customers—a man named Jacob Davis—who was using rivets to strengthen the pants he made. Davis was seeking a business partner to help launch his concept, and Strauss eagerly agreed.

In 1873, the two were granted a patent for rivet-reinforced pants—the very first blue jeans.

FEMALE POWER:
WOMEN OF THE GOLD COUNTRY

Lotta Crabtree

Lotta Crabtree

The mining camp of Rabbit Creek—later known as La Porte—produced its share of fortunes in gold during the early days in California, but its greatest contribution was a winsome little girl named Lotta Crabtree.

Lotta arrived in Rabbit Creek in 1884 with her mother, who opened a boarding house shortly after their arrival. As they settled into their new home, Lotta became mesmerized by the talents of Martin Taylor, a local saloon owner who entertained the miners by playing the guitar and dancing Irish jigs and reels.

Lotta often imitated his steps, much to the delight of Taylor. The more he watched her dance, the more he realized how uniquely talented she was. He decided to take her on as an informal student and help perfect her dancing skills.

One day, when a group of traveling entertainers arrived in Rabbit Creek, Taylor decided to put on a rival show. Lotta, of course, was his main attraction. Dressed in an all-green ensemble consisting of knee britches, tailored coat, and tall hat, she danced Taylor's jigs and reels, sang Irish ballads, and absolutely captivated the miners.

Given the overwhelming success of her performance, Taylor formed a troupe—with Lotta as the star—and toured the Mother Lode. She was always a hit with the entertainment-starved miners, and they showered her with gold.

Lotta Crabtree became the most beloved performer in the gold camps, and she ultimately moved to the East Coast to pursue an acting career. Her mother managed her enormous earnings, and much of the money went to charity and to building fountains. The most famous one is located in San Francisco and remains today as a monument to her glory.

Rosita

———◦○◦———

The story of a Scottish miner named Jack Caldwell and his Mexican fiancée, Rosita, is still remembered in the Mariposa County community of Indian Gulch.

On the day of their wedding, the church was filled with guests who were happily anticipating the marriage of the couple. When Caldwell failed to show up, a friend went to his cabin to track him down. He found signs of a bloody struggle, then soon discovered Caldwell's body at the bottom of a nearby mineshaft. He had been beaten and stabbed to death.

When Rosita heard the news that her husband-to-be had been slain, she was certain that the killer was a jealous former suitor named José. Vowing revenge, she rode on horseback to a secret cave that José had once pointed out as a hiding place of the bandit Joaquin Murrieta. It seemed a likely place for José to lay low, and Rosita was right.

"José, José," she called from outside the cave.

From inside came a voice, "My Rosita, my darling."

As José emerged, likely expecting a warm reception from the woman he loved, Rosita raised the gun Caldwell had given her and shot José dead.

After this harrowing experience, Rosita never married. She entered a convent, where she spent the rest of her life.

Jake's Betrothed

Money may not be able to buy happiness, but it can alter a man's future. Take the case of Jake, a lovesick young man from Oregon who was part of a prospecting party led by James H. Carson.

Jake had set off for California after the father of the girl he wanted to marry insisted that he have at least $100 before the marriage could take place. Determined to strike it rich, Jake was delirious with joy when his day's panning produced $500 in gold. He planned to return immediately to Oregon to marry, but his friends persuaded him to stay long enough to make additional money to set up housekeeping.

Three months later, Jake's haul had risen to more than $6,000. He bought some fine horses and threw away his buckskin suit in favor of expensive, store-bought clothes. When asked about his plans to return home to his prospective bride, Jake replied, "Well, I don't know as I'll go back to Oregon. And as to the gal, she's good enough—but her dad is pretty darned poor. I think I can do better somewhere else."

Bubbling Billy's Bride

The story of a miner called Bubbling Billy is something of a legend in the Mother Lode town of San Andreas.

Billy headed to California during the Gold Rush, leaving his new bride in the East. Like so many men before him, he promised to send for her as soon as he made his fortune.

Billy's luck in the goldfields proved fruitful. He made enough money to build a little cabin, where he planted a garden. As soon as his homestead was ready, he sent for his bride.

On the day she was due to arrive, Billy boarded a stage to meet her in San Francisco—and was never heard from again.

Ten years passed with no sign of Billy or his bride, and a young couple eventually moved into Billy's old cabin. One day, when the husband was cleaning out the spring in the badly overgrown garden, he pulled up some deep-rooted fern and a rusted old can came up with it—dripping water, and pure gold.

The townspeople agreed that this was a case of finder's keepers. They knew that Bubbling Billy, wherever he was, would be glad to see the couple get off to such a fortunate start with fifteen pounds of virgin gold—gold that Billy had hidden for his bride and never claimed.

Sisters of Mercy

Life in the Mother Lode was a grueling and dangerous one. Some men died in mining accidents. Others were murdered by their fellow miners. Men and women alike were victims of fatal illnesses and diseases. In all cases, they left behind countless orphans. Thanks to Reverend Thomas J. Dalton, the needs of these children were met—and met well.

In the late summer of 1863, he facilitated the journey of several nuns from County Cork, Ireland, to Grass Valley, California. The role of the Sisters of Mercy was to establish a local branch of their order and to tend to the basic needs and education of the orphans.

Dalton soon began construction on a combination convent/orphanage. A three-story building, it included sleeping quarters, lavatories, classrooms, a chapel, dining room, kitchen, laundry, parlors, library, infirmary, and storerooms. Named the Sacred Heart Convent and Holy Angels Orphanage, it was in operation from 1866 until 1932.

Masquerading Ladies

Women were in short supply in the Mother Lode mining camps. In fact, in many of the camps, there were no women at all. In spite of the absence of females, however, the Saturday-night dances still managed to be festive affairs.

The solution? Some of the roughhewn miners would obligingly play the roles of ladies. A piece of white-flour sack pinned to their coats was a sign that, for the evening, they were to be treated with all the gallantry and respect due to women. The other men were expected to ceremoniously ask them to dance, then pilot them gracefully across the crowded floor.

As a reward for their willingness to participate in this masquerade, the "ladies"—many of them bearded and bulky—were treated to free drinks at the bar.

ANIMAL MAGNETISM:
CRITTERS OF THE GOLD COUNTRY

The Jackass and the Bear

Excitement was in the air in Nevada City that spring day in 1851. Signs all over town proclaimed it was the day of a long-awaited battle: "A Fight to the Death between the Champion Jackass of the State and a Ferocious Grizzly Bear." The promoters claimed that the jackass had already beaten two bulls and a mountain lion in Sonora, so his lofty reputation heightened the anticipation.

A crowd of more than 1,000 miners was on hand for the battle. The electricity of the event began to fizzle somewhat when they saw that the heralded donkey appeared more unassuming than deadly as he ambled into the arena and began nibbling grass, his tail swishing at the occasional fly.

The bear, too, was a disappointment. Instead of a savage grizzly, he was a frightened, undersized cinnamon bear that had to be coaxed out of his cage. When the bear finally faced his grazing opponent, the jackass promptly thumped him with both feet and returned to eating grass. The terrified bear jumped over a nearby fence and disappeared into the chaparral.

"Hang the promoters!" the crowd yelled, but the fast-talking pair had quietly vanished.

To save the day, the miners spent the rest of the afternoon ferrying the donkey from saloon to saloon—pledging him as security for drinks, then taking up a collection to redeem him. When the miners tried to coax the donkey into joining them in their alcohol consumption, he stubbornly refused to drink anything stronger than water. As one miner later recalled, "That jackass was the only sensible one in the crowd."

Peggy, the Male Burro

Bill and Peggy were an inseparable pair around Knights Ferry in the days of the Forty-Niners. Bill was a prospector and Peggy was a burro—a male burro whose name derived from his peg leg. Bill had a special fondness for Peggy, due in part to the fact that he felt responsible for the animal's handicap.

As the story goes, he and his burro had gone to a gold claim where Bill wanted to set off a charge of TNT. When the explosive was planted, Bill ignited the fuse and turned to lead the burro away from the blast. When he didn't budge, Bill realized that the animal's steel shoe on his hind hoof was stuck fast to a wide vein of magnetic iron.

Bill had to think fast. He grabbed an axe and quickly chopped off the burro's foot, then dragged him to safety without a second to spare.

Bill nursed the animal for a full month, then replaced the missing foot with a wooden leg with a steel tip. Soon the newly renamed Peggy was ready for action once again.

Alas, this story was not destined to have a happy ending. One day, when Peggy was carrying a load of TNT, he lost his balance and fell 150 feet down a ravine. Bill hugged the rock wall as the resulting explosion shook the canyon—and sent poor Peggy to eternity.

During the time that man and burro were a team, Bill had always fared well with gold claims. After he lost his dear companion, however, his luck was never the same.

Abraham Thompson's Mule

A pack of mules idly grazing along a trail in the shadows of Northern California's Siskiyou Mountains was responsible for a mass exodus from the Mother Lode in 1851.

The creatures belonged to Abraham Thompson, a member of a gold-seeking party traveling overland from Oregon. The group had been prospecting, unsuccessfully, along the Klamath River. One morning, a few of the Oregonians started moving out after camping overnight in a meadow. Thompson opted not to join them, choosing instead to stay behind so his mules could feed.

As one of the animals pulled up a tuft of grass, Thompson noticed yellow flecks in the roots. He quickly panned out some of the dirt and found coarse gold.

"Come back. I've struck it!" he shouted, dashing after his friends.

Within six weeks, 2,000 miners had left the Mother Lode for this new settlement of golden promise. The area was named Thompson's Dry Diggings, which today is the town of Yreka.

Whiting's Dog Express

Supplying the mining camps of the Sierra during the winter months was one of the more difficult tasks of the Gold Rush. Although most of the camps were deep in the canyons and received mere flurries of snow, the trails leading to them threaded through ridges that were as high as 3,000 to 5,000 feet.

Because of the elevation, tall drifts frequently blocked the trails. In many instances, pack trains could not get through and miners were starved out of the canyons.

A man named Whiting, who hailed from Plumas County, finally came up with a solution. He trained teams of mongrel dogs to pull sleds over the snow—and his plan was a triumph. The dogs traveled into snowbound camps with little difficulty, delivering mail and supplies to the miners.

Word of the success of Whiting's Dog Express spread rapidly through-out the Sierra, and soon the barking of dog teams became a familiar—and very welcome—sound in the canyon camps.

The Tippling Rooster

One of the most popular early residents of the Mother Lode town of Indian Gulch was a rooster with a drinking problem.

The unusual bird first came to the town's attention when he hatched a nestful of eggs after the mother hen was killed by a skunk. The miners were so amused by the rooster's behavior that they adopted him as a drinking companion, feeding the creature crackers soaked in whiskey. Apparently the bird enjoyed these jaunts, imbibing with the men on a regular basis and living to a ripe old age.

The only downside of the rooster's drinking habit was the fact that, after his first spree, he never crowed again. The town's teetotalers contended that the poor bird felt too ashamed of his actions to ever make another sound.

The Meandering Cow

The Mother Lode town of Grass Valley, often considered the greatest mining city in the Far West, owes its birth to a wandering cow.

It was in October of 1850 that a miner named George Knight followed his wayward cow to a pine-covered slope. There, Knight stubbed his toe on a piece of quartz. His initial anger soon subsided as he examined the rock more closely. Momentarily forgetting about his cow, he rushed back to his cabin where he pounded the rock into dirt—and panned out a bright showing of gold.

After learning of Knight's discovery, a fellow miner searched nearby and found a small, gold boulder valued at $500. Word spread quickly, and soon the rush was on.

In seven years, Knight's Gold Hill Mine produced more than $100 million worth of the precious yellow metal—all thanks to George Knight's meandering cow.

Sacramento, the Wild Stallion

In the early days of California, bands of wild horses—ranging in numbers from 200 to 2,000—roamed the grassy plains of the San Joaquin Valley. They were noble animals, as fleet as the wind. One of the most magnificent of them all was Sacramento, a big, iron-gray stallion.

Sacramento had been reared by Captain John Sutter on his ranch along the Sacramento River. When Captain John Fremont made his first trip to California, Sutter presented Sacramento to him as a gift.

As time passed, the stallion was sent from Sonora to Monterey for service in Fremont's battalion. During the journey, the mounted unit was attacked by Spaniards. Sacramento performed gallantly, but his rider was killed.

After the Treaty of California was signed, ending the Mexican-American War, Sacramento was released from military service and sent by Fremont to a ranch for some much-needed rest and recuperation. On the way, however, he was stolen by Indians. True to his independent nature, he managed to escape and joined a band of roving wild horses.

Although many horsemen often attempted to catch this handsome steed, Sacramento always got the better of them and outran their horses. Clearly, he was a stallion who was meant to be free.

Coyotes in the Night

The man is nameless. His story was reported in the Special Historical Issue of the *Stockton Mail* on July 19, 1890. Although the journalist failed to record the man's identity, he captured the essence of an extraordinary night in 1840.

The hero of the story was a young trader in hides who often traveled to the San Joaquin Valley. As he settled in for the night during one of his journeys—his wagon and mules heavily loaded—he experienced a harrowing ordeal.

The spring evening was chilly, and the man knew he needed shelter. From a stack of flat, stiff hides, he pulled a few to fashion a shanty. Securing his makeshift structure, he placed a quarter-beef on its very top for future rations.

All seemed quiet as he bedded down for the night, snug in his house of hides. Suddenly, his sleep was shaken by howling coyotes around him and above him.

He related this detailed account to the Stockton Mail reporter:

"The pandemonium began. Snapping, snarling, and fighting, they were on the pile of hides, tearing at each other and the quarter of beef—rolling, tumbling. A mass of gray, four-footed devils. Every moment I expected that they would scent me, or that they would tumble my frail shelter around my ears. I had one shot in my gun, but what would that amount to?"

He lay perfectly still—certain that his skin house would collapse, waiting for what would surely be his death. Not only did the tiny house stand fast and strong, but the coyotes never found the man in the melee.

Just before daybreak, as early light brightened the sky, they slunk through the shadows to their lairs. The man crawled out from under his pile of skins to find the meat, including the bones, devoured. He hurriedly gathered his goods and broke camp.

Although nearly fifty years had passed between the incident and the telling of the tale to the newspaperman, the man was still frightened to think of it. Allegedly, he half-turned to the reporter, smiled, and said, "You notice that I've got tolerably bristly hair. It points in a good many directions, but mostly straight up. Well, I think it got in the notion of standing up that night. I presume it will never get over it now. I only wonder that it waited a few years before it turned white."

BAD GUYS AND WISE GUYS:
The Cruel, the Clever, the Cons

Black Bart

In the opening section of this book you met Charles Earl Boles, better known as the bandit Black Bart. Many stories still circulate about how he embodied the nature of a true gentleman, as reflected in this tale about the night he stayed in the Murphys Hotel under the name Carlos E. Bolton.

That memorable evening, a hotel guest from San Francisco, Mr. Wheeler, invited the scholarly looking Mr. Bolton to join him and two others in a friendly game of poker. By the time the game ended, Bolton had lost most of his money to Wheeler.

The following morning, Wheeler burst out of his room waving a gun in one hand and a note in the other. He confronted the hotel proprietor and demanded to see Bolton, but the innkeeper explained that he had left at daybreak. When he looked at the note that Wheeler finally handed him, he saw that it read:

"My Dear Sir:

May I take this opportunity to express my appreciation for an edifying evening in your company. I found the demonstration of 'the hand is quicker than the eye' most illuminating—but may I humbly suggest that when dealing from the bottom of the deck, it is unfortunate to be so placed at a table that a mirror, close by, reveals what is going on behind the scenes.

In view of the circumstances, I feel called upon to enter your room and relieve you of this evening's ill-gotten gains, together with such other trinkets of value as you may possess. In doing this, I take pleasure in demonstrating that 'the footstep is quicker than the ear.'
Faithfully yours,
Black Bart"

Brooks, the Teacher

Schoolteachers were scarce during the Gold Rush—so much so that when a gentleman named Brooks arrived in the mining town of Jenny Lind displaying a teaching certificate from an eastern college, he was hired on the spot.

After a week of teaching, Brooks borrowed a rifle from a hotel owner, Chester Jenkins, explaining that he wanted to go deer hunting for a little diversion. Instead, he strolled down the road and embarked on a new and more profitable career: he held up the stagecoach that ran between Stockton and San Andreas. With due consideration for Chester Jenkins, he left the man's rifle leaning against a tree before he made good his escape.

Once again, the town was looking for a new teacher.

Rattlesnake Dick

In 1856, the notorious Mother Lode highwayman, Rattlesnake Dick, began planning a robbery with five of his henchmen. The intended target was a mule train carrying $80,000 in gold from the rich mining town of Shasta to the San Francisco Mint.

At the appointed time, the gang members descended on the pack train on Trinity Mountain. They tied the mule drivers to trees and hurried off with the gold. When they arrived at their secret hiding place, they awaited the arrival of Rattlesnake Dick. Unbeknownst to them, however, Dick was in jail in Auburn for stealing mules.

After several days of waiting for the man who would never come, the bandits grew restless and quarrelsome. They began fighting among themselves, resulting in one's death. The remaining four buried half the loot and took off with the rest of the gold.

As they approached Auburn, a posse was waiting for them. A gunfight ensued, leaving one bandit dead and resulting in the capture of the other three. The posse recovered the $40,000 in gold that the thieves had with them, but the other half of the treasure still rests in that secret hiding place on Trinity Mountain.

The Pseudo Medicine Man

Medical treatment was hardly an authentic practice during the Gold Rush days. The fact that so many settlers survived is more a tribute to their hardiness than a testament to the quality of health care. In fact, a properly trained physician who traveled to San Francisco in 1851 reported that of the 200 doctors practicing medicine in the city, not more than thirty were genuine.

Saloonkeepers dispensed medicine and served whiskey over the same bar. Other bogus practitioners of the healing arts included grocers, gamblers, boarding house owners, and even shoemakers. So widespread was the ruse that many reputable doctors gave up their practices in disgust rather than compete with the charlatans.

Not all the imposters concealed their identity. One pseudo medicine man in the Mother Lode openly acknowledged that he was a quack. Amazingly, he continued to carry on a highly profitable practice.

When one of his "patients" developed a difficult-to-analyze fever, the faux doctor walked ten miles to another camp to seek advice from a genuine physician. Instead of being relieved when the real doctor confirmed his diagnosis and treatment of the ailing patient, the quack became highly indignant, writing in his journal, "That fixed him with me. I always knew he was an imposter."

The Crafty Landlord

The thousands of men who swarmed into San Francisco bound for the goldfields of the Mother Lode in 1849 and the early 1850s created a bonanza for hotels and boarding houses. The problem: many of the accommodations left much to be desired.

Some of them consisted of fifty or more canvas berths in a single room. Weary travelers would pay one dollar for a night's sleep—if they could manage to survive the onslaught of fleas.

One less-than-humane landlord had seven bunks but only one set of blankets, but he was not to be deterred by this lack of equality.

When the miners returned cold and tired after a day in the goldfields, they usually played cards for drinks before going to bed. When the landlord felt that a tenant was sufficiently warmed by the drinks, he would call him aside, escort him to the top bunk, then cover him with the blankets. As soon as the tenant dozed off, the landlord would remove the blankets and put them on the next bed. One by one, he would usher in all seven guests and repeat the process. Finally, he took the blankets off the seventh man and put them on his own bunk.

The following morning, he would charge his guests two dollars instead of one. When they complained, he would reply with great indignation, saying something like, "I ought to charge you more. I lost seven pairs of blankets last night!"

John J. Kelly

Like most men who arrived at the mines of the Mother Lode during the Gold Rush, John J. Kelly had his fears of the unknown. But even though his partner was killed in a mine explosion near Marysville, Kelly continued the underground mining that the two had started together—that is, until he encountered the world beyond.

Every night, Kelly religiously locked the door to the powder shack in the mine. Because the latch was inside the shack, Kelly had to slip his arm through a hole in the door to engage the lock.

On one fateful evening, Kelly reached through the hole and was traumatized to his core when a cold, clammy hand grasped his. He bolted from the mine, bellowing, "Me partner, me poor dead partner! He shook hands with me!"

Kelly wasted no time cashing in his gold and leaving the mine forever.

For years, the mine was considered haunted. Eventually, one of Kelly's friends admitted that he had been inside the shack with a bucket of cold water that memorable evening—and he just couldn't resist giving Kelly the fright of his life with an icy, wet handshake.

Despite Kelly's alleged encounter with the spirit world, he continued to hunt for gold for another twenty years, but he never again ventured underground.

George Gibbons and Tom Tomkins

Reliable mining partners were hard to find in the Mother Lode. But in spite of the odds, George Gibbons and Tom Tomkins crossed paths one day and became fast friends. Gibbons was a single man, and Tomkins had walked out on his bothersome wife. Together, the two men worked a profitable claim in Jackass Gulch near Tuttletown in Tuolumne County.

One day, Gibbons ran across a matrimonial ad in the newspaper. The prospective bride-to-be stipulated that her husband must not drink, gamble, or use profanity. Although Gibbons was known to indulge at times in all three vices, he replied to the ad with a glowing report of his honorable nature. It wasn't long before word came by return mail that his new bride was leaving immediately for California.

Tomkins knew full well that this marriage would mean the end of his partnership with Gibbons, so he acted quickly. When Gibbons left for San Francisco to meet his fiancée, Tomkins gathered up all their savings and purchased the Tuttletown Saloon.

When Gibbons and his drinking/gambling/cussing-hating lady arrived in Tuttletown, their stage stopped right in front of the saloon. Over the front door, Tomkins had erected a sign that read: "George Gibbons and Tom Tomkins, Proprietors."

Naturally, Gibbons lost his intended bride, who couldn't get out of town fast enough. In time, he learned to enjoy the saloon business, and it gave him some measure of satisfaction to know that his partner had been repaid for his prank. The wife that Tomkins had left behind in the East years ago finally caught up with him in Tuttletown.

Les Ingots

A close-knit group during the Gold Rush was a band of young Frenchmen known as Les Ingots. The money for their passage to California was raised by a lottery in France, and they made a point of reminding everyone of their roots. Although they spent time in the Mother Lode saloons, they never toasted anyone's success, refusing to buy drinks for others or allow anyone to buy drinks for them.

"We will do our celebrating in Paris," they always said.

It wasn't long before Les Ingots found rich gold deposits near Mokelumne Hill. Almost immediately, they announced that they had taken out a ton of gold and were returning to France.

Local hotel owner George Leger, a fellow Frenchman, gave the departing Ingots a gala going-away party. As the cavalcade wound through the streets of Mokelumne Hill on their gold-laden mules—singing "La Marseillaise," the national anthem of France—the Yankee miners sang back sarcastically:

"That's the way the money goes,

Pop goes the weasel."

Jim Townsend

The West had a generous supply of zany eccentrics during the gold and silver strikes. One of the oddest of them all was a newspaperman known as Lying Jim Townsend. Author Bret Harte—whose short fiction immortalized figures of the Gold Rush—is said to have modeled his character Truthful James after the truth-stretching Townsend.

Townsend was the editor of The Homer Mining Index, a newspaper owned by an English mining company in Lundy, a gold-mining camp in the eastern Sierra. Lundy was home to only a handful of businesses, yet Townsend's lively publication carried ads for three large grocery stores, a wholesale house, two banks, several saloons, and a host of other fictitious establishments.

The newspaper's social pages were filled with accounts of fashionable local events—a feat Townsend accomplished by copying stories from San Francisco papers and substituting names of local residents. And to round out the myth, The Index proudly proclaimed that some of the nation's foremost actors were appearing in Lundy's non-existent theatre.

All of these fabrications read well for the mining company's British investors, which was the primary intent of the ploy. Surprisingly, the local townspeople didn't seem to mind. In fact, many of them relished reading about the thriving, exciting place that Lying Jim Townsend had made of their humdrum Lundy.

The Fiddler and the Singer

Of the many duels fought in the early days of California, some had a lighter side.

In the Gold Rush town of Nevada City, two entertainers—a fiddler and a singer—got into an argument over the extent of each other's musical aptitude. Both agreed that the only way to determine who had the superior talent was to engage in a duel.

Entertainers were scarce in those days, and the townspeople feared losing one of them to this deadly contest. To ensure the safely of both men, while still preserving their honor, the locals hatched an ingenious plan.

On the day of the duel, the two men's seconds provided the pistols. Two shots rang out. The singer fell to the ground, his face a crimson mask. The fiddler ran to his opponent's side and began to weep.

"Poor feller," he cried. "He wasn't fit to die."

The singer jumped to his feet and demanded, "Who wasn't fit to die?"

It seems that the seconds had loaded the singer's pistol with powder, so his shot could not injure the fiddler. The fiddler's gun, which caused the explosion of red on the singer's face, was filled with nothing more lethal than a cartridge of currant jelly.

The Gambler and the Minister

It wasn't easy for the early ministers in the Mother Lode to find a sheltered space in which to conduct their services. As a result, it was often necessary for them to share a large tent that was also home to a bar and several card tables.

One Gold Rush miner recalled, "Often I have witnessed whiskey selling and drinking, preaching and gambling all going on in the same tent. It looked odd at first to see quiet men listening to the divinity of the word rise orderly from their goods-box seats, take a drink at the bar, then resume listening to the sermon."

On one occasion, a gambler, who was irritated with the preacher's voice, interrupted the services to offer the minister two dollars to cut his sermon short.

The minister meekly pocketed the money, declaring, "The Lord sent it, but the devil brought it."

His sermon continued uninterrupted.

The Greedy Saloon Owner

The early residents of the Mother Lode town of Volcano had an inventive way of coping with the rising cost of at least one commodity.

Word spread through town that the owner of a forthcoming saloon intended to lead a movement to double the price of a drink. On opening day, a large crowd gathered—prepared to take issue with the owner's inflationary tactics.

As soon as he announced his new price policy, the men in the crowd used poles to poke a large hole in the roof of the saloon, then boosted the terrified tavern keeper through the opening on the sharp edge of a ridgepole.

As he dangled there, he watched in abject misery as volunteer bartenders served free drinks to the thirsty multitude. Finally, the sight proved too much for him to bear, and he begged to be let down. The crowd released him after he solemnly vowed to never again tamper with the accepted price structure of alcohol.

Three Scheming Gold Miners

Not all prospectors who struck it rich during the Gold Rush made their fortunes mining. Sometimes, it was ingenuity that led to their success.

Take the case of three miners who tunneled into an unproductive hill near Jackson, California, in 1851. Frustrated by their bad luck, they decided to turn it into a bonanza.

Each evening, they conspired to pan out their day's digging just as the other miners were returning to camp. They consistently refused to show anyone the contents of their pans, and when asked if they were finding any gold, they would simply and reticently reply, "Not much." The secrecy of their actions caused the miners to assume that the tunnel was extremely rich.

To continue their subterfuge, the scheming trio ordered supplies from Sacramento: three large cook stoves, a long tent boarding house, camp stools, planks for tables, silverware, ten fat beefs, and a large supply of brandy. On the day the supplies were due to arrive, the three partners finally let the other miners see their pans. Each had been salted with about $500 in gold.

The news of a gold strike traveled rapidly, and everyone wanted claims near the tunnel. The threesome magnanimously obliged by selling fifteen-foot-square claims, with price tags as high as $300. It wasn't long before 3,000 gold seekers were swarming over the hill.

The trio that started it all was too busy running the boarding house and the tavern to be bothered working their claim. Of course, none of the other miners found any gold, and the camp was deserted within four days. Everyone agreed that the hill was worthless—except the three prospectors, who returned to the East with a tidy fortune.

John P. Jones

John Percival Jones arrived in the Mother Lode town of Weaverville, California, in the early days of the Gold Rush. He appeared to be a trustworthy sort, so a gentleman by the name of Farewell hired him to take care of his general store while he went on a trip to buy merchandise.

Soon after Farewell left, it began snowing heavily. Townspeople warned Jones that unless he shoveled the snow from the store's roof, it would collapse under the weight. Jones replied that he had been hired to tend the store, not to shovel snow.

One night, while Jones was sleeping in the store, the roof did, indeed, cave in. The snow blanketed the store's interior, and the worried residents began digging frantically. They called to Jones, but no reply came from under the white mounds.

When they finally reached him, Jones smiled up at them from his comfortable bed under the counter. He admitted that he had heard his rescuers calling him, but candidly explained, "If I had let you know I was all right, you might have stopped shoveling, and I would have had to clear out all that snow by myself."

As time went on, Jones continued to use his brain instead of his hands. He became one of the leading mining engineers in the Mother Lode, and also amassed a fortune in the Comstock silver strike in Virginia City, Nevada. He was later elected to the United States Senate and was responsible for many major developments in the West—including the city of Santa Monica.

Pike Sellers

Practical jokers were part of the fabric of the West during the Gold Rush, and Pike Sellers was one of the best. He earned his lofty reputation at Downie's Flat, near the headwaters of the North Fork of the Yuba River. The area was reputed to be incredibly rich, and news of its existence had spread far and wide in 1850.

When the first contingent of gold-seeking amateurs lowered themselves down the wall of the gorge to Downie's Flat, they were less-than-cordially greeted by Sellers and the other miners who had spent a hard winter in the camp.

When Sellers saw one of the newcomers approaching, he decided to have a bit of fun. He began furiously poking at the trunk of a jack pine, appearing to extract a gold nugget with every poke. As the tenderfoot watched in amazement, Sellers told him that the gold became lodged in the trees as they pushed up through the soil.

"Most of the big nuggets is up high," he explained.

The stranger quickly clambered to the top of the tree and began flailing away, much to the amusement of Sellers and the friends he assembled to watch this new high-altitude form of prospecting.

Forever after, the term "Jack Pine Gold" became synonymous with the inimitable Pike Sellers.

The Calistoga Con

Many wild tales about the abundance of gold in California circulated throughout the country. Some were probably true, others were completely bogus, and still others were wonderfully convoluted.

When *The New York Evening Post* reported about a strike in Napa County, Mark Twain couldn't help but chime in. The newspaper stated that the owner of a hot-springs hotel in Calistoga had extracted $1,060 in gold from ten barrels of spring water, using a method that only he knew about. Twain had mined in the Mother Lode long enough to know that the report was a hoax, so he wrote a letter to the newspaper claiming that he had owned those very same springs at one time.

"What surprises me," Twain wrote, "is the falling off of the richness of the water. In my time, the yield was a dollar a dipperful. It may be that the hotel proprietor's process is an inferior one.

"Mine was to take my uncle—I had an extra one at the time on account of his parents dying and leaving him on my hands—and fill him up, and let him stand 15 minutes to give the water a chance to settle well, then insert him in an exhausted retriever, which had the effect of sucking the gold out through his pores.

"I have taken more than eleven thousand dollars out of that old man in a day and a half. I would have held on to those springs, but for the badness of the roads and the difficulty of getting the gold to market."

LAW AND ORDER:
Peacekeeping Efforts

==>•<==

Extracting Confessions

The early-day miners in the Mother Lode had a favorite means of getting suspected criminals to confess. It may not have been the most civilized process, but it was usually effective. Their preferred solution: to fit a rope around the accused man's neck, then swing him off his feet a few times.

In most cases, the practice achieved the desired result in short order, and the hapless hangee would come clean and plead guilty. But sometimes, the outcome was much different than planned.

One day, a group of miners in the town of Oregon Bar tried the rope method to wring a confession out of a man named Walden, who was charged with stealing $100 in gold. After several unsuccessful attempts that left Walden swinging briefly in the breeze, they turned him loose. It was their hope that the poor man would lead them to the gold, but Walden would have no part of it.

When it was clear that he would not cooperate, the miners went after him with the rope once more. Exasperated, the neck-sore suspect declared, "If you're going to hang me, do it speedily and respectfully, without all this humbug, harangue, and torture."

Walden's words so shamed the miners that they reluctantly let him go. Whether or not he was guilty of the theft forever remains a mystery.

Administering Justice

Justice as we know it today is a world away from the methods that were utilized during the Gold Rush. Sometimes, the law of the land took a rather circuitous turn.

In one of the Mother Lode mining camps, a legal suit was brought by a miner called Shorty to recover the $40 he had loaned to a man named Green. Even though Green had struck it rich in the goldfields, he stubbornly refused to pay back his debt.

The judge ordered Green to pay the $40 as well as court costs, but that wasn't the kind of justice Shorty had in mind.

"May it please your honor," he began, "it ain't the money I want. If you'll just let me whale him, I'll forget the debt and pay the court costs besides."

The judge, startled at first, replied, "If the parties in this case want to compromise, let them do it."

With those words, Shorty proceeded to wallop Green while the judge stood by to make certain no one else intervened. The judge then ordered Green to pay the $40 claim anyway—plus court costs. Shorty got precisely the justice he wanted—and then some.

Judge James R. Reynolds

The judicial system during the Gold Rush was sketchy, at best. Mob rule and lynch law prevailed. Even judgments rendered from the bench were sometimes adulterated by whiskey, bribes, or emotions. Legal training was blinked at, and was often more imaginary than real.

"Judge" James R. Reynolds of Stockton was neatly interwoven into this questionable fabric. He was reputed to be more interested in self-service than justice, and a decision he handed down in one particular case triggered two murders and several hangings and fanned racial tension.

As 1849 was drawing to a close, a group of Chilean men had entrenched themselves high on a hill near the Mokelumne River. The area was undeniably rich in gold, and the men zealously guarded their claims. Their tactics included terrorizing any Americans who came close, but soon the latter had had enough.

They formed a delegation and tramped up the hill, ordering the Chileans to leave the hill. No arguments ensued; no protests arose. The Chileans held their tongues, much to the surprise of the Americans.

Nearly a week went by without incident. Then one night, the Chileans swept through the American camps, rounding up the miners. During the scuffle that followed, two Americans were killed and the rest were marched down a dark road leading to Stockton. One of the captives understood enough Spanish to learn that the Chileans were operating within the law. They possessed a blanket warrant—signed by Reynolds—that ordered the Americans' arrest. Apparently, Reynolds had appointed the Chileans as deputies, giving them the power to serve and execute the writ against his own countrymen. To this day, no one knows why.

When the men and their captors stopped for the night, the Americans managed to free themselves. They stealthily secured the Chileans' firearms, then woke them with punches and kicks. The tables were suddenly turned as the Americans led the bound Chileans down the same road toward Stockton.

Along the way they met the Stockton Rangers, who were on a rescue mission after hearing about the outrageous miscarriage of justice. A miners' tribunal was convened on the spot, and the men identified as the killers of the Americans were summarily hanged, others flogged, and two deprived of their ears. From that day forward, animosity between the two factions never cooled.

When Reynolds heard of the turn of events, he and his deputy fled Stockton in a rowboat, bound for San Francisco and anonymity.

Mob Law

The Mother Lode was home to courtrooms. And judges. And rules of common decency. But there was also the insidiousness of mob law.

One day, a young miner—who steadfastly refused to reveal his name— was arrested for stealing a horse. Although he denied the crime, a jury selected by an enraged mob preferred to believe the circumstantial evidence against him. He was speedily convicted and sentenced to hang.

Even on the gallows, the man would not reveal his identity, explaining, "You mean to hang me anyway, and I don't want my mother to know how I came to my death."

Two days after the hanging, the real thief was caught in the act of stealing another horse. His capture so stunned the town's honest miners that they made a vow on the spot: no man would ever be convicted by mob action in their town again.

The actual thief benefited from the earlier miscarriage of justice. Instead of being hanged—and in the absence of a penitentiary—he was sentenced to work on a chain gang.

A Hanging with Heart

Although mob justice ruthlessly prevailed during the Gold Rush, there were times when the law of the masses was carried out with a bit of compassion and heart.

A widower, the mother of two small children, was accused of murder. A mob jury found her guilty and condemned her to hang. The sentence was carried out as decreed—with one small difference. A box was fastened to a nearby tree and labeled "For the Orphans." Before day's end, it was filled with a small fortune in gold dust, placed there by the very men who carried out the woman's execution.

A Lynching Legacy

Punishment for crimes was usually swift and severe in the mining camps of the Mother Lode. Sometimes, however, the guilty-as-charged left behind a little bit of themselves.

Two young men, ages twenty-two and twenty-seven, were arrested as suspects in the burglary of a miner's cabin and a clothing store in the town of Murphys in 1852. When they were apprehended, the older one dropped a bundle containing some of the stolen loot, so a conviction happened in record time. The very next day, a jury of miners sentenced the pair to be hanged that evening at 5 o'clock.

In the brief time remaining before the ruling was to be carried out, the younger prisoner wrote a letter to a friend. It states simply:

"Dear Friend, I take this opportunity of writing these few lines to you, hoping to find you in good health. Me and Charley is sentenced to be hung today at 5 o'clock for a robbery. Goodby. Give my respects to Frank and Sam and Church."

This brief missive is now preserved in the San Andreas Museum.

Joyriding

Even in 1851, high-speed traffic in the young city of Stockton was beginning to pose a problem. In fact, the issue was so prevalent that the city council established a five-mile-an-hour speed limit on horse-and-buggy travel on city streets and prohibited riding on sidewalks. Each offense resulted in a fine of $25.

Try as they might, however, the authorities had little control over transportation speeds. By the 1880s, joyriding in buggies and wagons was so popular that police began winking at nag racing in the less-populated sections of the city.

Certain roads—including California Street and southern streets near Charter Way—became loosely sanctioned raceways where a shiny new buggy, pulled by a spirited horse, could be tested and raced. Some of the speeders included the cream of Stockton's high society, such as doctors, political figures, lawyers, judges, and even the town constable.

Crime and Punishment

Law enforcement in the mining camps of the Mother Lode was sporadic, at best. In spite of the lack of organization, however, thievery was not as widespread as one might imagine. For the most part, prospectors could leave their tents—containing gold and other valuables—unattended all day while they worked their claims.

It was common knowledge that thieves would be punished promptly and harshly for their crimes. No time was wasted on legal formalities, such as warrants, indictments, and appeals.

In one camp, two men were apprehended for stealing. One received 100 lashes as punishment. The other was given 250 lashes—and died of his wounds.

On the North Fork of the American River near the settlement of Coloma, a man who stole $300 had his ears amputated and the letter T, for thief, branded on one cheek.

But in yet another camp, crime was virtually nonexistent. The miners' law was posted and well understood: punishment for a first offense was a flogging, a second offense resulted in having both ears chopped off, and a three-time thief was summarily hanged.

A PLACE TO CALL HOME:
MINING CAMPS AND TOWNS

Jackson's Saloon, Escalon, circa 1895

Escalon

The hardships of trying to carve out a new future in the virgin land in southeastern San Joaquin County seemed overwhelming to John Wheeler Jones in the 1870s. Defeated and discouraged, he offered a steamship company all of his holdings in exchange for a ticket back to his native South Carolina.

Fortunately for Jones—and the community he would ultimately create—his proposition was refused. He returned to the land with renewed determination, armed with a grudging tenacity that would ultimately lead to success.

Jones eventually developed a town that grew up within the family's holdings. When his son, James, was trying to select a name for the town, he consulted the Stockton Public Library. He finally decided on Escalon, the Spanish word for "stepping-stone," to symbolize the stepping-stone the land had provided his father in building a community that would benefit so many.

Strawberry

———————

Most of the stopping-off places along the road between Placerville, California, and Virginia City, Nevada, had names indicating their distance from Placerville. One of the most popular spots, however, reached a bit deeper for its identity.

In the late 1850s, a man named Berry set up a one-room shack where he sold food and drink to travelers. Over time, he added sleeping quarters to his services.

Berry's offerings to customers also included hay for their animals. While this might have been a profitable endeavor, Berry miscalculated how much product he might need. During his first month of operation, business was so brisk that he ran out of hay and could offer only straw.

To clarify, hay refers to the entire harvested plant—including the seed heads—and is used as animal feed. When the seed heads are removed, the remaining hollow-tubed stalk is straw, which is typically used for animal bedding. Straw is the more inferior product, yet Berry charged the same price as he did for hay.

From then on, Berry's establishment and the surrounding Sierra meadow became known by a name that both identified the resort's founder and reflected his frugal nature: Strawberry. The area still bears that name today.

Grass Valley

The winter of 1852 was a stormy one in California's Sierra foothills. The town of Grass Valley was completely cut off from surrounding cities by wet roads, and supplies were running low.

Eventually reduced to short rations, the miners called a meeting to try to find a solution. In spite of their best efforts, they failed to come up with any viable ideas. Their only option appeared to be waiting until the roads dried out—a conclusion that heightened tempers and shortened fuses.

The miners erroneously blamed their misfortune on people, rather than Mother Nature. Impassioned speakers called for action against what they termed "the hoarders of Sacramento and San Francisco." A hastily formed committee on ways and means recommended a formal declaration of war on San Francisco and resolved, as the committee put it, "to get supplies peaceably if we can, forcibly if we must."

Fortunately, the storms subsided and the roads became passable before any action could be taken. The citizens of San Francisco never had to do battle with the militant miners of Grass Valley.

Hornitos Plaza, 1928

Hornitos

The Wickedest City in the Mother Lode—this is how Hornitos was known in the 1850s. The town's original settlers were gamblers, dance-hall girls, and troublemakers cast out of nearby Quartzburg, then a thriving gold camp.

The founders made their own rules, which were much looser than those in other communities. It quickly became a hideout for outlaws, including the notorious Joaquin Murrieta. Ironically, when the gold mines played out in Quartzburg, its straight-laced citizens reluctantly moved to Hornitos, where rich gold deposits had been discovered.

Originally called Hornitas, the name changed in 1877 to Hornitos, the Spanish word for "little ovens." The name derives from the town's Mexican tombstones that were shaped like small bake ovens.

Jenny Lind

---◆●◆---

The origin of the name of the town Jenny Lind is still debated today in this quiet little Calaveras county community.

Romanticists contend that the famous Swedish opera singer Jenny Lind, known as the "Swedish nightingale," gave her name to the town after performing there in the early 1850s.

The more reality-based folks argue that Jenny Lind never appeared west of the Mississippi River during her two-year stay in the United States, which lasted from 1850 until 1852. Rather, they claim that the name has its origin in two sources: the town's founder, Dr. John Lind, and the large number of pack mules, called jennies, that were constantly in the vicinity. Whatever the basis of the town's name, it is agreed by both factions that Jenny Lind is infinitely more melodic than the settlement's original moniker: Dry Diggings.

Yorktown

The prosperous Tuolumne County mining camp of Yorktown, near Sonora, found itself in dire straits in October of 1849. Gold continued to be plentiful enough, but the town's supply of liquor was completely exhausted.

After several seemingly endless days, an itinerant merchant arrived on the scene with a wagon loaded with barrels of whiskey. To no one's surprise, pandemonium broke loose. Scores of men scurried toward the wagon, carrying kettles, skillets, coffee pots, even tin plates—anything that could possibly hold several splashes of alcohol.

For three days, mining was virtually suspended. As one local miner later recalled, "Nearly all of our fellow citizens became mellow citizens. Whiskey was king." Loosely referencing the surrender of British General Charles Cornwallis at Yorktown, Virginia, in 1781, an event that marked the end of the American Revolution, he added, "Another Yorktown surrendered to Corn-wallowers."

Hangtown

In their hurry to start panning for gold, the early settlers of the mining camp of Hangtown—later to gain respectability under the name Placerville—put up their tents, shacks, and cabins wherever it was convenient.

When the town had grown to a settlement of about fifty dwellings, one of the miners discovered gold in the dirt floor beneath his makeshift home. He quickly began to dig down to bedrock, which touched off a veritable stampede as others did the same. Cabin sites were attacked with no mercy as the miners sought their fortunes.

As one English visitor to Hangtown recalled, "I went to the cabin of my friend, the Doctor, which I found in a pretty mess. The Doctor had a party of miners at work inside of his cabin on half shares. There were two large holes, six feet square and about seven feet deep. In each of these, three miners were picking and shoveling or washing the dirt in rockers. They took about a fortnight in this way to work all the cabin floor and found it exceedingly rich."

The City of New York of the Pacific

The City of New York of the Pacific was the lofty name given to the new community at the confluence of the San Joaquin and Sacramento rivers.

The year was 1849, and the town's ambitious founders were Colonel J.D. Stevenson—leader of a New York volunteer regiment that came around Chile's Cape Horn in 1847 to guard the newly acquired territory— and Dr. W.C. Parker, who accompanied him. Together, the two men made plans to create a metropolis that would rival its eastern namesake. They even offered the city as the state capital, but Monterey was chosen instead.

For a while, the new town prospered as a busy supply port for sailing vessels. But when steamships eliminated the need for frequent stock-ups, the City of New York of the Pacific rapidly disappeared from the map.

In 1862, the community came to life again under the name New York Landing, serving as a shipping point for the coal discovered in the foothills of Mount Diablo. Sadly, this resurgence was short-lived, and the town returned to slumber three years later when higher-grade coal was unearthed to the north in Washington and Oregon.

A new community, Pittsburg, was finally born on the old town site in 1909. The name was selected as a tribute to Pittsburgh, Pennsylvania, because of the steel and mining heritage shared by the two locales. At the time, the name of the eastern city more commonly appeared without the "h," which explains the spelling difference.

Auburn

The early citizens of the Mother Lode community of Auburn were an enterprising lot, even if they played by a questionable set of rules.

In the spring of 1850, the townspeople decided that Auburn should be the county seat of Sutter County, which then included much of Northern California. They contended that Nicolas had been the county seat long enough, and it was time for their town to have its moment in the spotlight. They raised such a fuss, in fact, that an election was called on the issue.

The promotion-conscious citizens of Auburn spread the word far and wide that free refreshments would be served on election day in the town's biggest general store—which just happened to be the local polling place. Their public-relations efforts paid off, and the news drew voters from as far away as Coloma. It made little difference to Auburn's boosters that Coloma was in the neighboring county of El Dorado. In their opinion, a vote was a vote no matter where it came from.

The results of the campaign far exceeded expectations. Auburn won by a majority larger than the county's entire population. This so impressed the town's rivals that when Placer County was formed, Auburn was selected as the seat of government with no contest at all.

William Brown and family, Modesto, 1871, Courtesy of McHenry Museum, Modesto

Modesto

Officials of the Southern Pacific Railroad were reaching the point of desperation the day they decided to name a new Stanislaus County settlement.

The railroad, which owned the community, had called a meeting of all the town's residents to select a name. Many of the suggestions proposed naming the town after a local dignitary, but to no avail. One by one, the leading citizens declined the honor of having the region bear their name. The railroad officials unanimously agreed: certainly such a display of modesty should be reflected in the town's name. And so the fledgling settlement was given the name it still bears today: Modesto.

Cowboys in Los Baños, 1904

Los Baños

One of Central California's oldest communities owes its development to cattle baron Henry Miller, who saw great potential in the broad plains at the base of what is now Pacheco Pass. But it was a Spanish missionary who is responsible for the community's distinctive name.

Whenever he traveled between Mission San Juan Bautista, where he was assigned, and the settlements of the San Joaquin Valley, Padre de la Cuesta often stopped in the area to bathe and refresh himself in a cool creek. It was only natural that the trading center that grew up around this pleasant oasis should bear the name he gave the stream: Los Baños, which means "the baths" in Spanish.

Ford's Bar

———————

Ford's Bar, on the Middle Fork of the American River, had the reputation of being one of the toughest mining camps on the river in 1849.

Having had their fill of lawlessness, the resident miners decided that the frequent brawls needed to stop. They got together and agreed on a few simple rules to secure the peace and quiet of the camp. The resulting code of laws called for the trial of certain specified offenses, but the system was not without its flaws.

The first case tried under this new policy involved a miner who had struck a man with a bottle. The other man retaliated by drawing a knife and inflicting several cuts on the bottle-wielding miner. Both men were arrested and taken before the magistrate.

Because the new code had no law against using a bottle as a weapon, the miner—who was the instigator of the fight—was acquitted. His victim was convicted of unlawfully drawing a knife, an offense that was expressly forbidden in the simple code.

One can't help but wonder how many more miscarriages of justice were carried out before the law was changed again.

Utica Mine surface works near Angels Camp, circa 1885

Utica Mine

Charles Lane, superintendent and part owner of the Utica Mine in Angel's Camp, was certain that the mine's true potential had never been tapped. Although several attempts had been made to develop the claim, they all ended in nothing more than meager success or complete failure.

The mine stood abandoned and unworked for years, but still the feeling haunted Lane. Sure of his convictions, he took a sample of the mine's ore to a San Francisco fortuneteller named Mrs. Robinson.

Upon examining the samples, she closed her eyes and uttered this message from the spirit world, "Deep in the earth where this rock came from lies gold—gold enough for a Croesus [the Ancient Greek king renowned for his wealth]."

That was all Lane needed to hear. He returned to the mine and ordered his men to sink the shafts deeper. One day, the Utica's shrill whistle was heard across the town. At 550 feet, the crew had tapped a vein of gold yielding $200 to the ton.

Lane was not even remotely surprised. He said he knew he would strike gold. A ghost had told him so.

Port Wine

It was in the early 1850s that a party of restless gold prospectors set out from Downieville, California, to investigate the mountainous region along the Yuba River.

During their exploration, one of the more venturesome miners stumbled on a cask filled with port wine hidden on the steep side of a canyon. It was likely cached there by a provident trailblazer who intended to retrieve it at a later date.

With the discovery came a sudden disinterest in prospecting as the men clustered around to sample the cask's contents. The more wine they drank, the thirstier they became.

Driven by a need for water, one of the prospectors slid down the precipitous slope to the bottom of the canyon in search of a stream. He found one—and also much more. The banks of the trickling stream were lined with fat gold nuggets.

Appropriately, the camp that quickly sprang up in that golden canyon was named Port Wine.

Lost Cement Mine

The Gold Rush had its share of lost mines, and one of the most famous was the Lost Cement Mine of Mono County. Tales of this fabulously rich strike had a small army of prospectors scouring the area for more than twenty years.

As the tale was told by Mark Twain, it was in the early 1850s that three gold-seeking German brothers were resting in a canyon in Mono County when they discovered a vein of cement shot full of lumps of dull yellow metal, which turned out to be two-thirds pure gold. They loaded up with samples, covered up the vein, and drew a map so they could find it again. They then took off to the Mother Lode for supplies.

The trip was a grueling one, and two of the brothers died en route. The third arrived so worn out that he never ventured back to claim the mine. He turned over the map and a vein sample to a man named Whitman, who spent the rest of his life searching for the mine without success.

Mark Twain claimed he saw the sample and said it contained "lumps of virgin gold as thick as raisins in a slice of fruit cake."

The miners in search of the Lost Cement Mine never fulfilled their quest. But in the process, they founded several prosperous camps in the High Sierra and opened up a scenic wonderland that is known today as Mammoth Lakes.

STRIKING IT RICH:
Good, Bad, and Accidental Luck

Sierra Streams

It was no surprise that James Marshall found gold nuggets so easily in the tailrace of Sutter's Mill on the South Fork of the American River. Millions of them were embedded in the streams of the Sierra Nevada—deposited in sandbars and eddies by raging rivers over a period of hundreds of millions of years. Early prospectors needed only frying pans, shallow bowls, and knives to free their fortunes.

By late 1848, 6,000 gold miners were working the rivers and creeks of the Mother Lode. A year later, their numbers had swelled to 40,000. Yet another 40,000 men and a few intrepid women were making their way from Stockton, San Francisco, and Sacramento to seek their share of the bonanza.

Of course, the gold was not in endless supply. But even though hundreds of prospectors were realizing daily that the readily harvested nuggets were no longer in abundance, fortune hunters continued to flood into the already crowded mining camps. Contributing to the misconception were wild and unfounded tales told by those entrepreneurs who benefited from the mass migration.

Maps printed in France enticingly, albeit erroneously, depicted the San Joaquin River flowing through a gold-studded plain between the Sierra Nevada and the sea—a plain that the mapmakers insisted was regularly replenished with gold.

Easy Come, Easy Go

During the days of the California gold strike, fortunes sometimes changed hands in a matter of minutes.

One observer saw a young boy, no more than ten years old, arrive at a gambling table with a few dollars, run it into several thousand, then lose it with the turn of a card.

A young man from the East borrowed ten dollars and began playing faro bank, a late-17th-century French card game. He played all night and into the next morning, eventually winning $7,000. Thrilled with his earnings and resolving never to play again, he boarded the next steamer for home—$7,000 richer than many a miner who spent months toiling for an elusive fortune in the Mother Lode.

A Little Boy's Christmas

The tale of a miner's Christmas gift to his six-year-old son in 1850 is one of the more heartwarming stories of the Gold Rush.

The miner and his wife lived with their two small children in the mining town of Mud Springs, about eight miles south of Placerville. On Christmas Day, he gave his son a prospecting outfit, including a small pick, shovel, pan, and rocker. Early the next day, the youngster announced to his parents that he was going to strike it rich. He marched off to an abandoned claim about 100 yards from the family home.

Before long, the boy excitedly returned to the cabin and showed his mother a lump of gold about the size of a kernel of corn.

"Go back and see if you can find a bigger one," his mother said, laughing at his enthusiasm.

A half-hour later, the child was back, beaming and bearing his latest find. It turned out to be the largest lump of gold ever found in Mud Springs, and it sold for $500.

Bob, the Servant

Most of the young men who sought their fortunes in the gold fields of California were a free-spending lot. One of them was a servant for Reverend Walter Colton, the Alcalde of Monterey, who was a judge, sheriff, and governor over much of Northern California.

Known only as Bob, the young employee carefully saved the wages he received from the reverend. He allotted himself only about twelve and a half cents a week for tobacco, keeping the rest of the money in a pouch sewn into the lining of his coat.

Lured to the mines by gold fever, Bob eventually left the alcalde's employ. Two months later, he returned to Monterey with $2,000. He rented a suite of rooms in the town's best hotel, purchased several fine horses, and hosted lavish parties. Before long, Bob had squandered the $2,000 and was leaving for the mines again. Reverend Colton happened to run into him just before his departure.

"I hope you haven't spent the savings you had sewn into the lining of your coat, Bob," the alcalde said.

"Oh, no, sir," came the reply. "I have that money yet. I worked hard for it and the devil couldn't get it away. But the $2,000 came easily by good luck—and has gone just as easily as it came."

Tom Carkins

In the 1850s, the Calaveras County mining town of Lancha Plana was home to Tom Carkins. He was one of the community's better-liked characters, although he was viewed as a determined cuss. On one memorable occasion, the measure of that determination was demonstrably evident.

Carkins, who was usually an amiable nipper, exceeded his limit of alcohol one night and attempted to tear apart the Golden Eagle saloon. The rampage resulted in his arrest and a sentence of thirty days in jail.

Furious, Carkins vowed to escape. With nothing more than a jackknife, he began digging a tunnel under the jail wall. This was a formidable task, given the fact that the jail was built of stone, and the wall extended four feet below the hard-packed clay floor.

He worked every night, through to the wee hours, until he was bone weary. Finally, after a particularly exhausting spate of digging, he saw that the end of his tunneling was near. He was certain that one more night of work would do it.

Tattered and dirty, he crawled into his bunk and sank into a deep sleep. He was still sleeping the following morning when the door to his cell opened and several of his friends burst in, shouting, "Wake up, Tom, you're a free man. Your thirty days have been served."

Bill Snyder

One of the hardest hard-luck stories to come out of the California Gold Rush was the tale of a miner named Bill Snyder.

Snyder had a rich placer claim on Oregon Creek near Camptonville in the Northern Mines, where he had taken out more than $30,000 in coarse gold. Just as the claim began to fail, he contracted dysentery. It was clear that he had to get to a doctor in Nevada City, roughly twenty-five miles away.

His primary concern was what to do with his gold, since he was too weak to take it with him. One night, as he stood outside his cabin in the moonlight, the solution came to him.

At exactly 10 pm, the moon cast the shadows of two sugar pines in a large "X" on the ground. Snyder decided to bury his treasure where the shadows crossed. When he returned from Nevada City, he would be able to locate his gold and dig it up at precisely the same time of night.

With great effort, he buried his fortune and headed south for treatment. It was six months before he was well enough to return home—where he received the shock of his life.

Where Snyder's cabin once stood was a looming sawmill, and every tree in the area had been cut down.

Folks said that before Bill Snyder went to the poor farm, he almost went to the asylum.

"We figured he was plumb crazy wanting to dig and putter around under those sawdust piles."

Dick Fellows

—⟫●⟪—

Dick Fellows would likely have gone down in Gold Rush history as a notorious stagecoach robber had it not been for his incredibly bad luck—and his inability to stay on a horse.

Several times, Fellows had meticulously laid plans for holdups—only to have them foiled by getaway horses that either threw him at critical moments or galloped off at the sight of him, particularly when he was toting a heavy strongbox taken from a stage. On one occasion, he fell into a mineshaft and broke his leg when a horse deserted him after a holdup. Following a series of fiascos, the last straw finally occurred in the late 1870s—putting an end, at last, to his zany career as a thief.

Fellows had been plying his nefarious trade in the Santa Clara Valley, where he was captured twice and escaped both times. When fleeing from the law the second time, he made the mistake of jumping on a horse that had been feasting on locoweed, a poisonous plant that causes, among other things, erratic behavior in livestock. When the bucking bronco was finally through with him, Fellows was happy to surrender.

After a hapless career, he ended up serving a life sentence in Folsom Prison.

Mike Callahan and Aubrey Osgood

Mike Callahan and Aubrey Osgood were unlikely mining partners. Callahan was a husky, hard-drinking man from Ireland, while Osgood was a frail, book-loving Easterner.

The two met on the ocean voyage from New York to San Francisco. When Osgood fell ill with fever during the overland trip across the Isthmus of Panama, Callahan carried him for miles to a settlement where he could get medical aid.

They finally arrived in the Mother Lode in August of 1850, staking a claim along the Cosumnes River south of Hangtown and building a cabin there.

Callahan's wealthy parents kept him well supplied with money, which allowed him to spend most of his days in his preferred pursuit: drinking whiskey. The majority of Osgood's time was spent working the claim, but soon he, too, began to imbibe. It wasn't long before alcohol became his primary focus.

One day, Callahan found Osgood hanging from the limb of the lone pine tree near the cabin. The shock of his friend's death caused him to swear off drinking and work hard on the claim.

One night, during a severe storm, the pine tree where Osgood hanged himself toppled over. The exposed roots and earth revealed one of the richest pockets of gold ever found in El Dorado County. The Lone Pine claim brought Callahan a fortune.

THE DARK SIDE OF THE MOTHER LODE:

WAR, DISCORD, AND TRAGEDY

Miwok Native American tribe members Joe Arnott and family, circa 1940

Miwok Indians

Prior to the Gold Rush, the broad plains of California's Central Valley and much of the Sierra were the land of the Miwok Indians. Many of them resided in the area of Lockeford and Clements, and they lived peacefully with their neighboring tribes.

When the gold seekers arrived in 1849, they drove the Miwoks from their homes and burned their villages. Not content with destroying the tribe's habitat, the miners hunted them down and massacred them in great numbers.

It wasn't until scores of years later that the Miwok leaders were able to get any restitution from the American government. Chief William Fuller, the son of an Indian princess and an Irish-German miner, was the foremost of these leaders. As the result of his tenacity, he managed to obtain the Cherokee Rancheria near Tuolumne for his people.

Chief Fuller was chairman of the Federated Indians of California, which was established in 1946 to seek payment from the federal government for lands taken from the Indians. In the interim, he sold his ranch in Twain Harte—a community named after two famous California authors: Mark Twain and Bret Harte—and used most of the money to help his people. When he died in 1958, the California State Senate adopted a resolution honoring him for his tireless work on behalf of all California Indians. Sadly, he did not live long enough to see the claim for restitution finally settled in 1968 for $29 million.

Yokut Indians

Among the tribes that shared the great San Joaquin Valley with the Miwok Indians were the Yokuts. They, too, were victims of the invading miners' viciousness, although they held on somewhat longer. When the Spanish arrived in the valley, about fifty tribes of Yokuts inhabited the area from Bakersfield to Stockton.

Many of them were taken away to the missions, and those who remained were either killed or died of diseases brought to their homeland by their Spanish conquerors.

As one historian explained, "The white man took his weaker brother's birthright and left him a pottage of war, disease—and death."

The Battle of Waterloo—California Version

In the stillness of that November night in 1861, a band of ten settlers stole the old cannon from Stockton's public square and silently loaded it aboard their horse-drawn wagon. Their plan: to use the ceremonial firing piece to fight San Joaquin County's very own version of the Battle of Waterloo.

Early the next morning, the cannon was moved closer to its target, a ten-by-twelve-foot fort built by John Balkwill, a young Canadian wagon maker. Balkwill had stocked his stronghold with food, ammunition, and a variety of firearms to enforce his claim to the land near Waterloo. The settlers would have none of it and wanted him out.

And so the battle ensued. The cannon boomed four times, but its aim was off. Balkwill fired five rifle shots, breaking the index finger of one of the cannoneers. A deputy sheriff eventually arrived on the battlefield and arrested the settlers for riotous conduct. Balkwill, who later retained part of the land through court action, remained immune inside his fort.

The historical, if nearly bloodless, Battle of Waterloo was over.

The Civil War in the Mother Lode

In the Gold Rush town of Volcano, California, there were strong feelings for both the Union and Confederate sides during the Civil War.

As the story goes, the town's Union sympathizers learned of a plan by the Confederate supporters to gain control of Volcano and divert the region's rich gold supplies to the Southern cause. Acting quickly, the Union forces decided on a show of strength to quell the uprising.

They wheeled into play a forbidding-looking cannon, which they fondly called Old Abe. In the absence of conventional ammunition, they gathered up large, round stones smoothed by the river and stacked them beside the cannon. The dramatic display of armaments had the desired intimidating effect, and the battle ended without ever beginning.

The Volcano War

Although the town of Volcano easily made it through its own version of the Civil War, such was not the case between the miners and the Sierra Indians.

Gold was plentiful and easy to find in the area, so the two factions worked amicably side by side. This harmony continued until one summer day in 1849, when a miner couldn't find his pick and claimed that an Indian had stolen it.

The chief, anxious to preserve the peace, assured a threatening group of miners that, if the pick was in his camp, he would return it. As he hurried off to investigate, a former Texas Ranger named Rod Stowell misinterpreted the quick move and shot the chief. As soon as the Indians learned of the shooting, they prepared for war.

To cover his blunder, Stowell and his cronies told the other miners that the Indians had attacked them and murdered one of their men. Outraged, the miners stormed the Indians' stronghold and chased them out. One miner was killed in the brief battle.

Later, when the miners learned that the Stowell group had lied about the cause of the trouble, they ran the rogues out of the camp. It was a classic case of too little too late, because the Volcano War had already taken its toll in human life—and a broken peace.

Farmers vs. Miners

———⟫•⟪———

Few battles in the history of California were so fiercely waged as the one between the farmers of the Central Valley and the hydraulic miners.

Using high-pressure jets of water, the miners ripped into the Sierra mountainsides, cutting through to gold-rich bedrock. Their success—enhanced by the fact that their methodology was relatively easy—lured other miners from their waning placer claims.

But soon the lower reaches of the rivers began to fill up with silt washed down from the hydraulic mines, causing disastrous floods every winter. In protest, the valley's farmers banded together to fight for legislation to prohibit hydraulic mining. The powerful mining companies organized their forces, as well, and both sides spent staggering sums of money before the Anti-Debris Act was passed by Congress in 1883.

In spite of—and in defiance of—the ban, some companies continued hydraulic mining, operating in the winter when the natural discoloration of the water would mask the tailings. When deputy sheriffs investigated the illegal operations, they were met with sniper fire.

But in the end, the law prevailed. In January of 1884, the Sawyer Decision—rendered by Judge Lorenzo Sawyer—stated that the practice must stop. Although an entire population of miners moved out, they left behind dying towns and horrific scars against the once-green mountainsides.

Indians vs. Miners

The Indians of Northern California's Trinity Alps resented the invasion of their mountain domain by gold-seekers during the 1850s. In retaliation, they raided the miners' pack trains and camps, slaughtered the miners' horses, and sometimes killed the men, as well.

One miner who stopped off at a mountain camp for the night awoke the next morning to find nothing left of his mule but the skeleton.

Another miner, who had been warned about the Indians' proclivity for thievery, slept one night with his mule's tether rope tied to his wrist and his pistol within easy reach. The following morning, the rope was undisturbed, the mule and the pistol were gone, and the man's blanket had vanished. Clearly, stealth was one of the attributes the Indians possessed.

Racial Tensions in Sonora

In 1850, the California state legislature passed the Foreign Miners Tax Law, imposing a tax of twenty dollars per month on all miners who were not citizens of the United States. The oppressive charge affected hundreds of Mexican miners who were working in the town of Sonora, and racial tensions escalated.

When a rash of murders occurred following the passage of the law, the American miners blamed the Mexicans. Four were arrested when a group of miners found them burning a tent in which the bodies of two men were found. In their defense, the Mexicans claimed that the dead bodies had been in the tent for several days, and they were merely cremating them.

The case went to court, and during an adjournment in the trial, an angry mob seized the prisoners, tied ropes around their necks, and propelled them off to a grove of large oak trees. Just as one of the men was about to be hoisted into the air, the judge and the town sheriff rode up. While the magistrate pleaded with the crowd to release the defendants, the sheriff and his deputies snatched the ropes and rode off, the prisoners running behind them.

The trial resumed, generating even more crowds than before. Rumors quickly spread that vengeful miners planned to attack any Mexicans they could find, so a sheriff's posse took 110 Mexicans into protective custody. Finally, a doctor who had examined the two bodies in the tent confirmed that the pair had been dead more than eight days before they were burned. The four Mexicans were acquitted, and the courtroom crowd grudgingly dispersed.

War Among the Chinese

On July 4, 1854, the California town of Weaverville—one of the wildest camps in the Northern Mines—was the scene of a full-fledged war between two segments of the Chinese community. One group was from Canton and the other from Hong Kong.

Blacksmiths and merchants all over town were tangentially involved, supplying the combatants with spears, pikes, tridents, tin helmets, and iron shields. Eager for any kind of entertainment—and apparently battles were deemed a recreational diversion—the local miners awaited the clash with amused anticipation.

After much beating of gongs and tooting of horns, the two opposing forces came to blows in a field near the town. The Canton army appeared to be winning when the tables suddenly turned. By pre-arranged signal, a band of American miners joined forces with the Hong Kong warriors and drove the Cantonese from the battlefield.

By this time, the festive spirit had taken a dramatic turn. Eight Chinese men and one American lay dead.

As one miner later recalled, "We thought the whole thing would be a farce, but the play turned into a tragedy."

Noonday Mining Company

The miners in the Gold Rush town of Bodie, California, were a free-spending lot—except for one man from Czechoslovakia who was employed by the Noonday Mining Company.

Lacking faith in Bodie's banks, the man refused to deposit his paychecks. Instead, he hid them away every month and lived as cheaply as possible. His plan was to make his fortune in the mines, then return to his homeland to live in luxury. Alas, his dream would never be realized.

The Noonday Mining Company eventually failed, leaving the stunned miner with nothing but worthless scraps of paper to show for his years of hard work and frugal living.

Bill Howard

Captain Bill Howard served with distinction and courage in the Mariposa Battalion in the Indian War of 1851. Later, he was placed in charge of an Indian reservation. While serving in this capacity, he saw the chief of the tribe about to throw a baby into the rushing waters of a river.

Howard rushed to stop the chief, who explained that the baby boy's mother was unable to care for him. Motivated by compassion for the child, this man who had slain scores of Indians in battle took the baby to raise as his own.

He named the child Ned and took him to Mariposa County, where he bought a cattle ranch. By the time Ned reached his eighteenth birthday, Howard had become a deputy sheriff.

Although Ned was raised to respect the law, he joined a band of cattle rustlers led by a man named Queue. They participated in several raids, and on one occasion, Queue began planning the theft of Bill Howard's prized cattle. He ordered Ned to lead the assault.

Ned immediately informed his father of the plot, then told Queue he would never steal from the man who raised him. Enraged that Howard had Ned's allegiance and he did not, Queue killed the young man in cold blood.

After a brief trial, Queue was acquitted and set free. Bill Howard lived to the age of ninety-eight, but he always held in his heart the memory of the son whose loyalty to family could not be disputed.

Modoc Indians

Of all the Northern California tribes, the most feared by the gold miners were the Modoc Indians. In 1852, after the Modocs murdered the occupants of an emigrant train, a volunteer company was formed to hunt them down.

When the effort failed, the group resorted to trickery. Using the services of a messenger, they invited the Modocs to peace talks—then promptly and deliberately killed them.

A few years later, the score was somewhat evened.

Captain Jack, the Modoc chief, and his tribe were battling American soldiers at what is now Lava Beds National Monument in Siskiyou and Modoc counties. The chief invited the opposing general to a truce conference and killed him—a deed for which he later paid with his life

Michael Brennan

For many, the quest for gold in the Mother Lode was heartbreaking. For some, it was downright tragic—and Michael Brennan was among the latter.

He and his family arrived in Grass Valley from New York City to take possession of a mine that Brennan had bought. At first he was successful, but his gold-bearing vein soon began to falter. He launched a frantic search to relocate it, but it proved to be elusive.

Brennan returned to New York to raise more money to continue his relentless pursuit. In time, he exhausted every source of additional capital and finally gave up. Defeated and despondent, he slayed his family and killed himself.

Not long afterward, other miners discovered the lost vein just a few feet from where Brennan had stopped work. A fortune was taken out of the mine that had brought death to an entire family.

*Received Sonoma 20th May 1848 of L.W. Boggs
Twenty five Dollars on account of the late Scott
William L Todd
For painting the Famous Bear Flag
The above named William L Todd is the Person
who painted the famous Bear Flag at Sonoma 1846
and is his own hand writing*
W. H. Boggs

Probably the only existing relic of the famous "Bear Flag" — — which was
destroyed with many other invaluable relics of California's early days
in the great San Francisco earthquake and fire — is this receipt for
the money paid William L. Todd for its painting. The receipt bears every
evidence of authenticity. Todd has been generally accredited with the
painting of the flag; W. W. Scott was a member of the revolutionary party;
and L. W. Boggs was alcalde at Sonoma during 1848.
    This receipt was evidently presented to the San Joaquin Society of
Pioneers — probably in the 60's — and was firmly pasted on the inside
cover of a scrap-book for preservation. This statement of particulars is
made in case the authenticity of the receipt is questioned at any future
time.

Jan 2
1932

Harry Noyes Pratt
Director
PIONEER MUSEUM
HAGGIN GALLERIES

June 2, 1932

2.

Bear Flag document, Courtesy Haggin Museum, Stockton

The California Flag

The three dozen Yankee trappers and setters were sorely in need of a flag
that June day in 1846. They had just captured Sonoma, the northern
outpost of Mexican California, and were proclaiming California an
independent republic. To create the proper impression over the vanquished
Mexicans, a distinctive new banner had to be raised—and raised quickly.

From homespun cloth and a strip of flannel from a petticoat, they
fashioned a reasonably presentable flag on which they painted a red star.
The group felt that it still needed an animal that typified California, so
they chose the grizzly. According to one trapper, "It's a bear that always
stands its ground."

The defeated Sonomans thought the crudely painted bear looked more
like a pig. But to the thirty-six proud new Californians who cheered as
the flag was raised, the banner represented the dawn of a new era in the
history of the West.

FROM HERE TO THERE:
Travel and Transportation

Getting to the Gold

For Easterners traveling to California, the journey during the Gold Rush was perilous. Although overland trails were ten thousand miles shorter than the trip around Cape Horn in South America, the land had fewer chartings than the high seas.

Gold seekers from New England favored ships, but passage was long, costly, and uncomfortable. Those who chose this means of transportation claimed it was preferential to the Forty Mile Desert—the name given to the Lahontan Valley in Nevada—which was renowned for being hot, waterless, and profoundly treacherous.

The Isthmus of Panama provided a latter-day shortcut via riverboat or highland mule—a journey that took five days and was fraught with grave dangers, including malaria and cholera. And once on the west side, travelers had to wait for weeks until passage up the Pacific Coast could be secured. The ancient sailing vessels were slow, rickety, and obliged to head far out to sea before winds carried them landward to San Francisco.

In spite of the hardships...in spite of the risks...the quest for gold had an unwaveringly strong attraction. Turning a deaf ear to the voice of reason, hundreds of thousands of individuals headed off into the relative unknown in their search for fortune.

First High Sierra Crossing

The first crossing of the High Sierra by men seeking to make their fortunes was not from east to west as one might suppose, but from west to east. Jedediah Smith first accomplished this feat in the spring of 1827.

Smith and a party of trappers were searching for new sources of beaver pelts when they took off from Utah and headed to Southern California, following a route south of the seemingly impassable Sierra. The Spanish governor of San Diego ordered Smith and his group to leave California by the way they had come, but Smith was not about to be told what to do. Instead, he and his men traveled north into the San Joaquin Valley, where they found beaver.

Smith, along with two others, left the party in the valley to return to Salt Lake. Twice they tried unsuccessfully to cross the Sierra—once by way of Kings River, then via the American River—but the snows were too deep. The men and their horses nearly froze to death.

The last desperate attempt was made up the Stanislaus River near what is now Ebbetts Pass. By the time they tried this route, the snow was well packed and the party made it through in a week.

In time, other intrepid travelers opened trails through the great mountain barrier, but Jedediah Smith was the first to prove it could be done.

The Mail Must Go Through

Mail service left much to be desired in the Mother Lode during the early 1850s. It was not unusual for three months to go by before a steamer finally appeared in San Francisco with bulging bags crammed with letters and newspapers.

As soon as word of its arrival spread, a mob of people anxious for word from home descended on the city's post office. Harried clerks would lock the doors and work through the night, feverishly sorting the mountain of mail.

The anxious crowd never dispersed. Instead, they waited impatiently for the doors to reopen, sometimes threatening to storm the building.

When the sorting was finished, the postmaster would order the crowd to form a line before the mail would be delivered. The hastily formed queue would stretch for several blocks, and some opportunists made a living selling their places in mail lines.

The men in the mining camps didn't always have the luxury of traveling to the city to get their mail. Instead, they often relied on private agents who transported correspondence from the San Francisco post office to the mines. Taking full advantage of the situation, these go-betweens charged as much as a dollar per letter for their delivery system.

Messenger Service

Before stagecoaches became common on the trails of the high Sierra, communication between mountain camps and the Central Valley was entrusted to a rather primitive service. Messengers traveled by horseback in the summer and on snowshoes during the winter, and the latter means of travel was particularly perilous.

In January of 1860, a story in The Sierra Democrat, the Downieville newspaper, described one such journey:

"On Thursday morning while Joe Blodgett was on his way from Sierra City carrying the mail, he was attacked by eight wolves and was obliged to drop the letter bag and his rubber coat, which were unceremoniously chewed up and scattered. He lit some pitch pine and made all the noise he could, but the brutes would not leave him until they had eaten his lunch and spare clothing."

Road Hazards

The adventurers who passed through San Francisco bound for the gold mines of the Mother Lode were confronted by particular difficulty during the rainy season. Because of the lack of drainage facilities, the city's streets from November through May were seas of mud—mud so deep that people actually drowned in it. To travel at night on foot without a lantern was to court disaster.

Although lumber would seem to be a practical solution to the problem, its price of $600 per thousand feet made it far too costly. Residents tried everything they could think of to create some sort of fill—often dumping large tree branches into the mud—but this proved largely ineffective. As they constantly sought new options, one neighborhood came upon a highly creative—albeit less than perfect—solution.

They filled one section of road with sacks of flour, another with large boxes of tobacco, and still another with cooking stoves. The stove lids were not always securely in place, so pedestrians had to be particularly vigilant.

The most precarious streets were usually posted with signs to warn travelers of the dangers ahead. One particularly treacherous road bore the message:

"This street is impassable.

Not even jackassable."

Steamship Sagamore built for Weber, docked in Stockton Channel, 1851

The First Paddlewheeler

On November 15, 1849, the first paddlewheeler thrashed its way through Stockton's murky water. It was named the John A. Sutter, after the man for whom a youthful Charles Weber had worked as a fort foreman.

All of Stockton turned out to see this extraordinary vessel, piloted by Captain Warren. Whistles blew and bells rang as the stern-wheeler eased to an embankment and tied up to an old oak tree.

A gangplank was tossed ashore and guests filed aboard, welcomed by the captain with a river of champagne. There wasn't a sober male in Stockton that night.

Captain Warren's generosity bore ample dividends, because soon the *John A. Sutter* became a floating goldfield. After just a few months of shuttling goods and passengers between Stockton and San Francisco, the good captain was able to log a highly respectable $300,000 to his bank account.

Riverboat Passage

The overnight trip from Stockton to San Francisco by riverboat was an unforgettable experience for travelers in the mid-1800s. Several stately paddlewheelers made the run over the years, and many were built on the Stockton waterfront.

A typical journey went something like this.

Every night at 6:00, a husky whistle signaled the departure of one of the boats. Passengers loaded up, crowding the rails and watching as the dome of the Stockton courthouse disappeared in the distance. Soon the view was of levees and fields, highlighted by the twin purple peaks of Mount Diablo looming beyond.

Children and adults alike watched with fascination as the boat's massive paddlewheel churned the river to foam. Sacks of flour were stacked on the freight deck, destined for San Francisco. A whistle signaled a stop at a small wharf to pick up additional bags of potatoes and grain.

In the boat's dining room, passengers could watch the passing landscape as they enjoyed oysters and other gourmet delights. Anyone craving a full turkey dinner could purchase one for fifty cents. After an evening of conviviality, they climbed into their bunks to be lulled to sleep by the rhythmic turning of the paddlewheel. The next morning, the boat docked in San Francisco, where passengers spent the day exploring the majesty of the city.

An exciting era came to a close in the 1930s, when the romantic riverboats gave way to more modern, faster means of transportation.

Stagecoach Competition

———————

Competition among various stage companies carrying passengers and freight over the Sierra during California's early days was bitter—and often brutal.

Drivers would try to ram the wheels off a rival stage if they happened to be lucky enough to encounter one on a bad turn. Those who had the wall side on a grade would relish the opportunity to crowd a competitor off the other side.

The passengers were invariably the hapless victims of this reckless and dangerous behavior, and they usually suffered in silence. But sometimes, one would rise up in wrath.

Such was the case at a station in Marysville, where a stage was changing horses. A rival stage arrived on the scene, and its driver began circling the stationary stage, knocking off spokes and other equipment.

After the second round, an irate passenger poked his head—and a shotgun—out of the stage window. He fired off a series of shots that killed the aggressive driver. A jury subsequently acquitted the passenger of a murder charge, calling it a case of self-defense.

Charlie Parkhurst, Stage Driver

One of California's best-known stage drivers in the 1800s was a character named Charlie Parkhurst. A loner and a quiet sort, Parkhurst serviced regions throughout the Mother Lode.

One passenger, J. Ross Browne, reminisced about a ride he took with Parkhurst from Sacramento to Placerville in 1869. He admitted that his mind kept racing with stories about holdups, stages crashing into canyons, and horses becoming entangled in harnesses and overturning coaches.

But in spite of his fears—regardless of the foul weather and bleak night—Browne proclaimed, "I had a implicit confidence in Old Charlie. The way he handled the reins, and peered through the clouds and volumes of darkness and saw trees and stumps and boulders of rock and horses' ears—when I could scarcely see my own hand before me—was a miracle of stage driving."

Upon hearing this, Parkhurst replied that the sound of the wheels indicated location. "When they rattle, I'm on hard ground. When they don't rattle, I gen'r'lly look over the side to see where she's going." The frequency of tobacco chewing was another sign of a perilous road. "When I'm skeered, I chaw more'n ordinary."

Parkhurst drove a stage for more than thirty years. With increasing age came rheumatism, aching knees, and the loss of an eye due to a horse's kick, but he continued to push on, embracing a lifestyle of "chewin', moderate drinkin', and a little dice-throwing for cigars."

Parkhurst eventually retired to a quiet little farm near Watsonville. The neighboring townspeople were friendly and generous, caring for him when he developed cancer of the tongue, which led to an agonizing death on December 29, 1879.

As friends were preparing the body for burial, they made a shocking discovery: Charlie Parkhurst was a woman. The fact was confirmed by a Watsonville physician, who added yet another piece of startling information: Parkhurst had also been a mother.

News of Parkhurst's true identity sped to every stage depot in the state of California. A story in the Yreka Union stated:

"More light may be thrown on this wonderful case. The female stage driver, Charlie Parkhurst, left $4,000.00 to a little boy who had been kind to her."

Today, the woman who elected to enter a tough segment of a man's world lies buried in the Odd Fellows' Cemetery in Watsonville. And with her is buried a multitude of tantalizing secrets.

Kansas to California

———✦———

The party of emigrants led by John Bartleson faced a crucial decision that September 15th in 1841.

Nearly five months had elapsed since their westward journey began in Kansas, and they had made it as far as the eastern slopes of the Sierra. Faced with the formidable task before them, they abandoned their wagons and assessed the situation. They knew that climbing the rugged mountains would be treacherous, and they could become trapped by early snow.

The diplomatic group cast ballots on whether or not they should turn back. By the slim margin of one vote, the decision was made to continue onward to California.

At the time, no one in the party could possibly know the far-reaching effect their balloting would have—least of all the young man from Germany who cast the deciding vote. He was Charles M. Weber, who later founded the City of Stockton.

John Bidwell

Missouri to California

The torturous overland trip to California was plagued by hardship and adversity.

Sixty-nine men, women, and children started the trek in Missouri in 1841. On the journey, nearly half of them broke away and changed their destination to Oregon. By the time the remaining members—led by Ohio schoolteacher John Bidwell—reached the sheer eastern flanks of the Sierra, they had forsaken their wagons and eaten most of their oxen.

Following the Stanislaus River, they drove themselves and their starving animals up seemingly impenetrable granite passes. They collected water in pans, kettles, and their boots, tipping it down the throats of their horses and oxen to keep them alive. For food, they shot and ate crows and wildcats.

Once the sun went down, the dangers escalated. Indians frequently stole and ate their horses. But still the emigrants pushed on.

One night while on a scouting mission, Bidwell stumbled against a huge fallen tree whose base towered twenty feet over his head. Later, he determined that he was the first pioneer to discover the Calaveras Grove of giant sequoias.

When the exhausted party finally reached the San Joaquin Valley, they feasted on antelope, sandhill cranes, and wild grapes. The double mountain dominating the pristine plain told them their ordeal was over. They had reached Mount Diablo, gateway to the Pacific Crest.

Boston and California Joint Mining and Trading Company

Some of the prospectors who arrived in San Francisco during the Gold Rush were affiliated with a company or association, so they shared the cost of chartering a ship and funding equipment. One of the wealthiest groups was the Boston and California Joint Mining and Trading Company, which sailed from Massachusetts in January of 1849 aboard the 700-foot Edward Everett. Among the elite party's 150 members were eight sea captains, a mineralogist, four doctors, medical and divinity students, merchants, artisans, and manufacturers.

The ship had no shortage of amenities. Accommodations included a large dormitory and social hall, and a band presented nightly concerts. A lecture series was conducted by scientists in their various fields of expertise, and prayer meetings were held on a regular basis.

The Edward Everett also carried enough food to feed the passengers for two years. With an eye on life in the new frontier, it also carried wheelbarrows, a wagon, several steam engines, two cannons, a lightning rod, and enough lumber to build company offices in San Francisco.

The buildings, however, were never erected. The company—like so many others—disbanded shortly after arrival in San Francisco. The stories of quick and easy fortunes were too tempting to resist, so individuals abandoned the company plan in their haste to find their own fortunes in the goldfields

LIFE BEYOND THE MINES:
Culture and Leisure Pursuits

Cultural Firsts

Volcano was as wild and woolly as any mining town in the Mother Lode, but it was also a cultural pacesetter. It was there in 1850 that Robert Beth, a man of refinement and education, helped establish California's first rental library.

Beth encouraged local merchants to provide books in their shops, renting them for ten cents a day. Four years later, the Miner's Library Association was formed, firmly establishing Volcano as a book-centric town. Joining the association cost one dollar, and monthly dues were twenty-five cents.

In that same year, Volcano recorded another cultural original: the establishment of the state's first little theatre group, the Volcano Thespian Society. The town's golden age had arrived.

Miners' Fashion Statements

Although photos usually depict gold miners as shaggy men dressed in rags and tatters, there was another side that echoed sartorial splendor. One visitor to the town of Sonora recalled that Sundays brought out all the swells dressed in varying degrees of foppery.

"Many wore red or orange handkerchiefs tied across their chests and hanging over their shoulders," the tourist wrote. "Some men wore flowers, feathers, or squirrel tails in their hats. Occasionally, a beard was worn plaited and coiled up or was divided into three tails hanging down to the waist. One miner with long hair brought it down each side of his face and tied it in a large bowknot under his chin."

In spite of the adversities of life in the mines, fashion was alive and well in the Mother Lode.

Gambling

As one might expect, vices were plentiful among the miners of the Gold Rush, but perhaps the most preferred of all was gambling. The card table captured the reckless spirit of the Forty-Niners—and most of their gold dust.

Throughout the mines, poker was the game of choice. Bets ordinarily ranged from one to six ounces of dust, although they sometimes escalated to heights of thirty-six ounces, valued then at about $576.

One night, in a mining camp on the Tuolumne River near Sonora, the pot in a poker game was growing mightily. One of the participants decided that he needed more gold dust to stay in the game. Pushing his stash to one side, he turned to a companion and said, "Watch my pile, friend, while I go out and dig enough dust to call that raise."

Language of the Gold Rush

The California Gold Rush and the hordes of multi-cultural groups that it attracted produced a unique vocabulary peppered with slang and profanity.

If a person was in a highly emotional state, he was said to have "the peedoodles."

A confrontation or disagreement was a "conbobberation."

To be intelligent was to be "ripsniptious."

A small fleck of gold was a "chipsa" or "spark."

Striking it rich was a "bonanza." The opposite was a "borrasca," the Spanish word for "storm."

It was the Mexican miners who spoke of the veta madre—the mother vein—when describing the golden stratum that extended from Mariposa to the Trinity Alps. The U.S. prospectors translated it to Mother Lode.

Some phrases that originated during the Gold Rush—such as "stake a claim," "see if it pans out," and "strike it rich"—are still deeply embedded in the English language today.

Made in the USA
Columbia, SC
23 July 2020